D1367547

hanu
stor

Frederick Fell Publishe
2131 Hollywood Blvd., Suite 305 • Holly
www.Fellpub.com • email: Fellpub

hanukkah
stories

Thoughts on family, celebration and joy

NANCY RIPS

Frederick Fell Publishers, Inc
2131 Hollywood Blvd., Suite 305
Hollywood, Fl 33020

Excerpt by Wayne Dosick from *Dancing with God: Everyday Steps to Jewish Spiritual Renewal*. Copyright © 1997, reprinted by permission of Harper Collins Publishers.

Excerpt by Ozzie Nogg, "The Cap Poppa Got from the Czar" from *Joseph's Bones: A Collection of Stories*. Copyright © 2004, reprinted by permission of Oznas Books.

Copyright © 2011 by Nancy Rips. All rights reserved.

All rights reserved, including the right to reproduce this book or portions thereof in any form whatsoever. For information address to Frederick Fell Subsidiary Rights Department, 2131 Hollywood Boulevard, Suite 305, Hollywood, Florida 33020.

For information about special discounts for bulk purchases, please contact Frederick Fell Special Sales via email: **fellpub@aol.com** or visit our web site: **www.fellpub.com**

Designed by Elena Solis
Manufactured in Canada

10 9 8 7 6 5 4 3 2 1

Library of Congress Cataloging-in-Publication Data

Hanukkah stories : thoughts on family, celebration and joy / [compiled by] Nancy Rips.
    p. cm.
 ISBN 978-0-88391-197-6 (cloth : alk. paper)
1. Hanukkah--Anecdotes. I. Rips, Nancy.
 BM695.H3H385 2011
 296.4'35--dc23

                              2011029965

ISBN 13: 978088391-197-6

To Noah

May you be like the spirit of Hanukkah,
lighting the darkness and making the world a better place.

As long as Hanukkah is studied and remembered,
Jews will not surrender to the night.

—*Rabbi Irving Greenberg*

On Hanukkah we say:

We thank you for the miracles, the triumphs,
the heroism, and the help you gave to our ancestors
in days past and in our own time.

contents

introduction

Hanukkah is the holiday that lights up our lives. It's one of the most joyously observed Jewish holidays because it takes place in the home with all of the generations celebrating together. And the only accessories needed are a menorah, a working match, and a lot of love.

Hanukkah is also known as the Festival of Lights because Jews all over the world light a candle on their menorah each evening for a total of eight nights. By doing so, we remember the brave Maccabees who redeemed and rededicated the Temple in Jerusalem thousands of years ago. Although the victors had only one night's worth of oil left for the sanctuary's eternal lamp, a miracle happened and after they lit the flame, the oil lasted for eight days.

The miracle of Hanukkah comes from the victory of the few over the many. A small group of Jews stood up to the might of the Syrian-Greek Empire and prevailed. This happens so rarely that it rates as a real miracle. In fact the weekly portion we read in the synagogue during Hanukkah proclaims: "Not by power nor by might, but by spirit". Each of us has the power to be that miraculous spirit to ourselves and to others, to light up the darkness and make the world a better place.

In *HANUKKAH STORIES*, over 101 people share their personal memories, tales and recollections. Some of the contributors are household names, while others are just like you and me. Their stories burst with tradition, love and hope and take us from an RV camp in California, to the ice in Finland, and even aboard Spaceship Hubble. The stories come from people of all ages, all walks of life, and all across the globe.

Hanukkah is a joyful holiday. It's a time to rededicate ourselves to family, celebration, and joy. And it's a time to share our stories and traditions with our loved ones today and our future generations tomorrow.

hanukkah
stories

I

A Great Miracle Happened There

*The meaning of Hanukkah,
the holiday that lights up our lives every winter.*

The greatest gift of Hanukkah may be our ability to recognize that miracles can happen for us. And the greatest miracle may well be the miracle of self renewal that is available to us all the time.

— *Rabbi Daniel F. Polish*

At this time of year, when the sun is most hidden, the holiday of Hanukkah celebrates the rays of hope and light. Indeed, the physical darkness of this time of year can be a metaphor for the darkness that often envelopes us at times of illness and loss of a loved one, when the world sometimes seems dark and cold. At such times, we yearn for the sun and the light and warmth it provides. Often it is through simple and unrecognized miracles that we are able to feel the warmth of hope and light.

— Rabbi Rafael Goldstein

* * *

I can't remember a Hanukkah without snow. Snow in drifts as tall as a man. And that man? My Poppa-the-Rabbi, trudging home from shul in the evening darkness to light the candles. Poppa with a wool muffler over his nose, rubber galoshes flopping on his feet, and his head warmed by a Persian lamb fur cap.

On any given Hanukkah night, Poppa would stomp into the house, blow the snowflakes off his cap and say, "So, did I ever tell you who gave me this cap?" He'd asked this question many times before, and of course I knew the answer. But pretending I didn't was part of our family's Hanukkah tradition.

"No, Poppa. Who gave you the cap?"

"The cap? The cap was given to me by Czar Nicholas, himself."

"Really, Poppa! When?"

"When I was seven, maybe eight. It was Hanukkah and Czar Nicholas just happened to be passing by our village when, through the open window, he heard me singing *Maoz tzuuuur y'shooo-a-seeeee*. He was very impressed."

"What did Czar Nicholas do then, Poppa?"

"What did he do then? He walked straight into our house, put the cap on my head, shook my hand and said, 'You may call me Nikki.'"

And from the kitchen Mama would yell, "*Oy*, Alex! Such stories you tell her."

The Hanukkah candles we lit when I was a child were fat, sturdy and orange. Not plain-Jane orange, mind you, but *orange*. And when those candles stood in the frosty window, their flames melting the ice until it puddled on the sill, well. . . anyone passing by knew he was looking at candles that meant business. *Don't mess with us*, they seemed to say, *if you know what's good for you.* Just like the Maccabees.

While the candles burned on those long ago evenings, I spun my dreidel and Poppa sang his Hanukkah songs, in Hebrew, Yiddish, Russian, English. I loved the singing, really I did, but Momma wouldn't start frying her *latkes* until the singing was over and the candles burned down to nubs, and sitting through Poppa's Hanukkah concerts in anticipation of those *latkes* wasn't easy. Mama's *latkes*, you see, were the true miracle of Hanukkah.

"And what makes the taste of Momma's *latkes* so miraculous?" Poppa asked every year.

And every year my response was the same. "The secret ingredient!"

I knew the answer, but pretending I didn't was part of the tradition. "Tell me, Poppa! What is the secret ingredient?"

Then Poppa would put down his fork, wipe the sour cream off his moustache, take momma's hand and whisper, "The secret ingredient is the tiny piece of her knuckle she grates in along with the potatoes."

Blushing, Momma would say, "*Oy, Alex. Such stories you tell her.*"

Growing up, I knew nothing about Hanukkah shopping lists or fancy wrapping and bows. And a gift every night? Never. I got one present and one present only. Hanukkah gelt that Poppa took from his trouser pocket and put, unwrapped, in my palm. Every Hanukkah the gift was the same. An uncirculated 1923 silver dollar that Poppa had somehow gotten his hands on the year he came to America. He kept a stash of these coins in a black wool sock hidden behind our stove. I don't know who he thought he was hiding them from. I knew where the treasure was. And Poppa knew that I knew. But pretending I didn't know was also part of our family's Hanukkah tradition. And we observed that tradition until the fateful Hanukkah of 1944.

It was the day of the fifth candle. We woke to find the

radio. . .gone! The Victrola. . . gone! In the kitchen, Poppa moved the stove. *Oy vey! Gevalt! Ganeyvim!* Unlike the small jar of oil that kept burning in the Hanukkah story, our seemingly inexhaustible treasure had vanished. Stolen while we slept by some non-sectarian Grinch.

I wept. Poppa fumed. Then he put on his coat and fur cap and marched straight to the bank. That night, as he had done for years, Poppa gave me my Hanukkah gelt. I turned the coin over and over, studied its face. It was familiar but somehow different. And then I realized what was wrong. The dollar wasn't engraved *1-9-2-3*. The numbers on this silver dollar were *1-9-4-4*.

"Poppa?"

"*Tochter.* See how it shines, so bright, so new. This new gift is much better than the old."

And Momma sighed, "*Oy, Alex. Such stories you tell her.*"

Looking back, I realize that a child more perceptive than I would have gotten a clue, right then, that more than just dates on silver dollars can change. Now, when I gather with my children and grandchildren to celebrate the

Festival of Lights, it's good, of course. But my Hanukkah is gone. It's been replaced by frantic shopping and a gift every night and candles that are thin, pale imitations of the real thing. Sadly, the *latkes* are often made from a mix. The snowdrifts are seldom tall as a man. And the singing rarely merits a reward from the Czar.

It's then I run back to a magical time. I taste my mother's latkes, hear my father's Hanukkah songs. I remember histories and feel the silver coins in my hand. These riches can never be stolen. They are secure, safe—along with the knowledge that hidden deep in the bottom of my dresser is the cap Poppa got from the Czar.

— Ozzie Nogg

* * *

The miracle, of course, was not that the oil for the sacred light, in a little cruse, lasted as long as they say, but that the courage of the Maccabees lasted to this day. Let that nourish my flickering spirit. *— Charles Reznikoff*

We're taught in the Jewish tradition the same story over and over. whether it's the Holocaust or the Maccabees, we have to rise above persecution and do our best. Just as magic is about making people dream, we learned to take things that aren't supposed to be and turn them into something beautiful.

— *David Copperfield*

Sometimes even Hanukkah miracles can happen to you.

When our youngest child, Leo, was a preschooler, he stayed a bit later at school on Wednesdays for lunch and an art class, which gave me a few precious hours on my own. One particular Wednesday, I planned to go to one of my favorite stores, Von Maur at the Westroads Mall. Von Maur is a throw back to the department stores of old, with great customer service and a wonderful atmosphere. But before I headed to the mall, I checked my e-mail.

I discovered there was to be a Hanukkah menorah lighting ceremony at the mall later that day, as well as a canned food drive. Ohhhh, I should go to that, I thought. It will be good for the kids to observe the holiday and also do a good deed, to boot. I decided I would push off goinguntil after school so that all my kids could join me.

The date was Wednesday, December 5, 2007. At 1:42 p.m. that day, a gunman opened fire, shooting innocent people at the Von Maur department store. Eight people, ages 24 to 66, were senselessly killed and others were seriously injured. It was one of the deadliest mall shootings in the United States.

I will never know for sure, but a part of me believes that I experienced my own Hanukkah miracle that day. As the gunman was heading into the store, with murder in his heart, I was safely on my way to pick up my little Leo on a cold, December afternoon.

— *Janet Kohll*

* * *

Hanukkah is more than a commemoration of the triumph of Judah Maccabee over the Syrian Greeks. In modern America, it has become one of the most important and joyous holidays of the Jewish calendar. It's a holiday for the whole family, celebrated at home.

— *Mae Shafter Rockland*

On Hanukkah, Jews are reminded to believe in miracles. We re-tell the story of the tiny vessel of oil that burned for eight days, and assure ourselves that when people have faith, anything can happen.

— *Zelda Rankin*

* * *

Hanukkah is the most widely known Jewish holiday, despite the fact that it is a minor holiday. Hanukkah is not described in the Torah, and it doesn't have the significance of Passover or the High Holidays. Still the celebration of Hanukkah, the history behind its traditions, and the symbolism of the menorah reinforce the basic tenets of Judaism: dedication, perseverance, generosity, and remembrance.

— *Synagogue Bulletin*

The first stamp released to mark the united states post office's holiday celebration collection celebrated Hanukkah. It was released in 1996 and announced jointly by the united states and israel. The u.s. stamp had the word "Hanukkah" in english while the israeli stamp printed the word in Hebrew.

— *Scott Strawn*

When I think about miracles, I think about this brand new grandson with the giant, wide-open eyes that I'm holding in my arms. What miracles await this little child? And what kind of man will be become? Will he be spirited and bright like my dad? Maybe he'll have my mom's great looks and quick-witted opinions. Or perhaps he possesses my twin brother's positive outlook of goodness and generosity? My older brother's sense of family history? Or my sister's eternal optimism? Maybe he'll embody my love of books and Judaism and music?

Oops. I forgot about the other side of the family.

— *Nancy Rips*

* * *

The miracle is not that one vessel of oil lasted for eight days, but that the community was willing to light one vessel not knowing whether it would last. The true miracle is daring to dream.

— *Bruce Feiler*

ב

Tradition!
Tradition!

*Stories of Hanukkah are passed from person to person,
home to home, generation to generation.*

Since 1999, I have had the privilege of representing the 9th Congressional District in the United States House of Representatives. I grew up in that district which includes the North Side of Chicago and some northern suburbs.

A few months ago, I appeared on a panel of legislators at Boone Elementary School, not far from the home I lived in most of my childhood. Boone housed the Sunday School of my synagogue because Temple Menorah in Chicago's West Rogers Park was too small to accommodate the number of children who attended each week.

When I walked up to the stage that evening and took my designated seat, I had a flash of a long lost memory. That stage was the site of one of my first successful performances in front a crowd, if you don't count my disastrous dance recital at age five. (But that's another story.)

Suddenly, it all came back to me. I had been chosen to recite the blessings over the Hanukkah candles at the big, holiday assembly in front of all the students and their parents. The auditorium, which seemed enormous to me back then, was over-flowing with people. I remember feeling excited and confident, but as a seven- or eight-year-old, I must have been nervous, as well. My singing was flawless. (At least I thought so!) Afterward, I luxuriated in the praise of my teacher and family and decided from then on that singing the blessings over the Hanukkah candles was my special talent!

Coming back to earth, the community meeting proceeded rather uneventfully, but I was smiling inside thinking about my special Hanukkah memory.

— *Congresswoman Jan Schakowsky*

* * *

May love and light fill your home at Hanukkah.

— *Synagogue Bulletin*

I close my eyes and think of Grandma tasting a bit of her childhood each Hanukkah when she prepared the latkes as her mother had made before her. My mother, my aunts, and mygrandmothers all float back to me, young and vibrant once again, making days holy in the sanctuaries of their kitchens, feeding me, cradling me, connecting me to the intricately plaited braid of their past. And even at this moment, looking down the corridor of what's to come, I see myself join them as they open their arms wide to enfold my children and grandchildren in their embrace.

— *Faye Moskowitz*

* * *

My favorite Hanukkah memory was never about presents. It was about family. Now with our son, Zev, we celebrate Hanukkah with renewed vigor. We play dreidel like poker. Just don't ask me to make latkes. I'm good at eating them, not making them.

— *Marissa Janet Winokur*

They called us Tom and Jerry. And just like the famous cartoon characters, my favorite cousin, Tom, and I were always in a little bit of mischief. Jewish holidays, when our families got together, were our specialties. We loved Hanukkah—the presents, the dreidel games, the dinners. When everyone was downstairs at the dining room table, we were upstairs checking out the traffic from Tom's bedroom window. No one even knew we were gone. And the best part was we loved being together.

Tom and I are still great friends looking for a little mischief.

— *Jerry Slusky*

* * *

We take our three boys to Children's Hospital every year, where we give the sick children bags filled with Hanukkah stickers, cookies, and dreidels. Our boys even donate some of their old video games. It makes us all feel good, especially the children at the hospital who enjoy the treats and their "new" video games.

— *Stacy Simon*

When I was a child, my parents started Hanukkah Theme Nights with our family. One night we got books as presents, another night was the dreaded pajama-and-socks night, another night we served dinner at a homeless shelter, and still another night we always went to the movies. My favorite night was when we would take a walk outside before lighting the candles. We'd talk about how cold and dark it was on wintry, December evenings. Then we'd come inside to light the menorah and bask in the glow and warmth of our home and our family. That was my favorite night every year.

— *Barbara Grossman*

* * *

When our boys were little, we decided to give them an envelope each night with money. The first one contained a dollar bill. We could see the look in their eyes, like, "That's all?" We told them to be patient and they wouldn't be disappointed. We planned to double the amount each night. They figured it out around Day Five. Then they were really excited!

—*Bobbi Leibowitz*

When my mom passed away just days before Hanukkah, one of the first things I did when I got up from sitting shivah was to get out her big box grater, pile potatoes on the counter, and start peeling. My tears started long before I even got to the onions, and that will probably be my experience again this year and every year from here on. But one thing is certain: for me, food, especially Jewish food, is intricately linked to the people we love, to tradition, and more than anything, to memories. Here's to honoring our memories.

— Lisa Kelvin Tuttle

Hanukkah is my favorite holiday because it's about joy and singing. As a child I always liked the idea that by lighting the candles we were symbolically bringing light to the darkness. My family and I would sing songs each night and add an additional candle until the final night, when all the candles were burning.

Now it's just my husband and me singing the songs alone. I remember when we were first married. We would look at each other and think it was a little weird. We don't do any of the other Jewish holidays alone, but there's something great about observing Hanukkah because it's such a warm festival, even if we're back to just the two of us.

— *Marion Baker*

When I was growing up, my mom's family had very little money. She taught us to play a dreidel game with walnuts instead of coins. The "walnut game" was played with a bag of walnuts and a slanted board. The board was placed against a chair and the walnuts were divided. Each player rolled a walnut down the board with the intent to hit as many other walnuts as possible. When a walnut touched yours, it would be added to your pile. The person with the largest walnut pile won.

It warms my heart to know that my grown-up kids still choose to play my mom's homemade dreidel walnut game.

— *Sandy Epstein*

Hanukkah was a wonderful time as a child in Sioux Falls, South Dakota. There were only fifty Jewish families out of a population of 50,000, and because of the generosity of our parents, we always felt a deep connection to both the Jewish and general community. Every year, mom made Hanukkah cookies and invited our classes from school over for a snack and to learn about our holiday. We wanted everyone to know who we were and why we believed what we did. Our friends were all impressed and respected us. One day for 'Show and Tell' I even taught my classmates a few Hebrew letters and words.

My brothers and sister and I got a present every night. We even thought pajamas and socks were great gifts!

We all learned an important lesson in Sioux Falls —whether one lives in a thriving Jewish community or a small one, the warmth and beauty of Judaism keeps us all together and gives us the strength to enjoy life and live it to its fullest.

— *Jeanne Shechet*

Growing up in Argentina, we did not celebrate Hanukkah as it is in December, which is summer and the end of the school year. As a rule, no liberal Jew in those days paid much attention to the holiday.

Even so, we began to celebrate Hanukkah after we got married because we wanted to make it meaningful and joyful for our kids. We started taking pictures of the children each year with the Hanukkah candles.

Now in America, we still light candles, but what I really love most is how we hug at the end.

— *Susi Frydman-Levin*

* * *

I grew up Jewish in a non-Jewish neighborhood. Although I had many shared interests with the other kids, when it came to the Christmas season, the similarity ended. Though I never said anything, my father could sense that I wished I could be just like the other kids who couldn't wait for that rotund and red-suited Santa Claus to climb down their chimneys and bring them tons of presents on Christmas day. Perhaps that is why he invented his own mythical counterpart solely for Hanukkah, whom he dubbed "Hanu-Claus." I was pretty young at the time, and so for several years, I believed that Hanu-Claus actually existed.

We did the traditional things on Hanukkah. We visited back and forth with the grandparents, aunts, uncles and cousins. My mother would make wonderful latkes, honey cakes, and every night we would light the menorah, play dreidel games, and on nights one through seven of the holiday, I would receive Hanukkah gelt, or chocolate coins wrapped in gold foil. But on the eighth day, I would get a big present, such as a wagon, a scooter, a toy kitchen set or a big doll who said "mama" when you tipped her forward and backwards. Those gifts supposedly came from Hanu-Claus.

Eventually, I reached the age of skepticism and discovered that those large presents wrapped in blue paper and silver bows and hidden in the back of the hall closet did not come from a mysterious benefactor named Hanu-Claus, but rather from my parents. But in order not to hurt my dad's feelings, I played along with the subterfuge.

I loved my dad. He could be an austere figure at times, but he had a wonderful sense of humor, and he taught me many things, including the Ten Commandments, which I learned when I was only four years old. He particularly emphasized the "Honor Thy Father and Thy Mother," commandment, which to this day has had a great impact on my life.

On one of my childhood Hanukkah mornings, I got up early and tiptoed to the living room where the anticipated gift was in its presentation place on the large, round coffee table surrounded by my mom's Hanukkah decorations. The house rule was to wait until my parents got up before opening the present from Hanu-Claus. I felt lucky that particular day because I didn't have to wait too long. They both wished me Happy Hanukkah with hugs and kisses and then headed to the kitchen for their morning coffee. All of a sudden I heard a scream and several "oy veys." I quickly rushed to the scene to see what was wrong. There, on the kitchen floor, were several inches of water. Where on earth had it come from? Mom and dad scurried about, grabbing lots of rags and a mop and pail, and kicked off their shoes. I just stood there, dumbfounded, but my dad had a knack of turning a preposterous situation into something logical. "Well, I guess since we don't have a chimney, Hanu-Claus had to come through the water pipes," he said, rubbing his chin as though he actually believed what he was saying.

I envisioned Hanu-Claus as being roughly the same size as Santa Claus, so I said, "That would have to be a miracle. Nobody could fit in those pipes."

My dad countered with, "Maybe it was a miracle. After all, Hanukkah is itself a miracle. How do you think the oil in the Temple burned for eight days when there was only enough to last one night?"

Mom, who was wringing out the mop, said in a sarcastic tone as she waded to the sink, "Here is your miracle. There are no broken pipes because I checked under the sink. The stopper was left in and the faucet was not completely turned off. It's a miracle, all right, that the whole house didn't get flooded and wash us all away."

Dad grinned sheepishly. He was the one who had washed the dishes the night before and unlike mom, had carelessly left the kitchen before making sure everything was unstopped and turned off. He apologized profusely, and had a way of eventually smoothing mom's ruffled feathers. In all the excitement, I totally forgot about opening my present, which turned out to be the dollhouse I had been coveting for months.

Now, many, many years have passed since that fateful Hanukkah morning, but the memory of it seems as clear as yesterday. Each year as I light the menorah, especially the last candle, I fondly recall my parents of blessed memory, the Hanu-Claus myth my dad invented, and of course, the kitchen sink overflow.

I like to think of that day as a miracle. It made me realize how precious and fleeting childhood Hanukkah memories are.

— *Gloria Shukert Jones*

* * *

He who has fed a stranger may have fed an angel.

— *The Talmud*

During the five years of the war, there were no Jewish holidays at all for me in the camps. That's why I was so happy to finally be living in Israel, because it was a dream come true. We had always dreamt about having a homeland of our own. I remember walking in the streets of Tel Aviv for the first time and seeing inscriptions in Hebrew. By the time I settled in Jerusalem, it was Hanukkah. In the windows of the stores there were menorahs. All of a sudden the memories from my childhood, from my grandmother, came back to me. All of a sudden I had to change my image once again. I no longer had to shed my Jewish girl for Polish girl. Now I had to crawl out from my Polish skin and crawl back into my Jewish skin.

— *Leah Hammerstein Silverstein*

One of my fondest memories of Hanukkah goes back to my childhood. My mother had a wonderful friend named Harriet who used to have a Hanukkah party for many children. Harriet didn't have any children of her own so I always thought this was especially nice of her. She would sit all of the kids down in front of her as she read Hanukkah stories to a fascinated audience. She used puppets to play the different characters and allowed our imaginations to fill in the rest.

After her presentation, this wonderful woman would have a gift for each and every child to open. She then treated all of us, parents included, to cake and candy as we all sang Hanukkah songs and played dreidel.

I have always cherished those times and when I became a mother and a grandmother, I have tried to follow her lead and host many Hanukkah parties, not just for my children and grandchildren, but for friends' children, as well. It makes the holiday special and memorable.

— *Marilyn Tipp*

My grandmother was born in Palmyra, Missouri. They were the only Jewish family in the town and her father wanted them to be aware of their Jewish heritage. He also wanted them to be able to attend a place of worship. So they celebrated every Jewish holiday in their home and then attended the Lutheran Church.

We moved in with her after my grandfather passed away. I was nine months old. When I was 13 and becoming involved in Jewish activities, I was no longer comfortable with the Christmas tree. We compromised and had a Hanukkah bush. Only blue and silver lights and blue and silver balls were allowed.

My grandmother loved being Jewish. She was president of the local Council of Jewish Women, but she wanted the fun of the other holidays, as well.

— *Joan Bernstein*

* * *

My biggest present is my family.

— *Joseph Katz, age 6*

Being a seven-year-old Jewish child in the Midwest, the Holidays were always fun but a bit confusing, too. At school everything was centered on Christmas: Plays, songs, cookies and decorations. There were only a few Jewish kids in my class and two of them were my best friends. At that time of year I moped about in junior drama-queen style, feeling sorry for myself. I told my mother that it was not fair that the Christian kids got to hang stockings and Jewish kids couldn't.

Well, finally mom and dad figured out a way to hang stockings on the night of December 24th with the focus on Hanukkah instead of Christmas. They told me there was also "Hanukkah Harry" for the good Jewish kids, too. Then they allowed me to invite two of my Jewish girlfriends to sleep over and hang stockings. It was the ultimate sleepover party. My brother, my friends and I each hung one of our knee-high stockings. Even Grandma Pearl brought over her pantyhose to fill.

The next morning we all woke up to find our stockings bulging with goodies. Even our dog had a stocking filled with dog biscuits! The stockings were filled with giant

Israeli Jaffa oranges, apples, nuts, candies and a special note from Hanukkah Harry that could only be read by putting it in front of a mirror.

For the next two years we hung stockings for Hanukkah Harry and took great delight in finding them filled the next morning. Then, my brother became religious and Hanukkah Harry never was seen again.

— Beth Brown-Gershovich

* * *

My own memories of Hanukkah are inextricably linked with my father's singing of *Maoz Tzur*, which means Rock of Ages.

My father didn't sing it the way it is taught in todays' Hebrew schools. His version is melodic and mournful, complete with crashing crescendos and lilting liturgy. It is emotionally evocative of both the highs and lows of Jewish history. He learned this melody from his father, who learned it from his father, who heard it from the Bluzhiver Rebbe, a Chassidic leader in Galicia.

My father taught the melody to his children and it became as beloved to us as it was to him. Growing up in Brooklyn, the highlight of our Hanukkah was gathering around the menorah as my father recited the blessings and then joining in as he masterfully sang "his" *Maoz Tzur*. My six brothers and one sister are all blessed with good singing voices and the resulting chorus was beautiful, indeed.

As the eldest in the family, I was the first to get married and move away from home. That first Hanukkah in Detroit, I was homesick for my father's *Maoz Tzur*. I called my mother and was told to hold on to the phone and listen as my father was about to light the menorah.

And so a tradition was born. Every Hanukkah, usually on the fifth night, I would call "home" and my children and I would listen as my father, and whichever siblings were there, would sing *Maoz Tzur*. As the years went by and there were grandchildren and great-grandchildren spending Hanukkah with Zeide and Bubbe, they, too, would join in the singing and the chorus continued.

Sadly, over the past several years, my father's health has steadily declined and I know that when I make that phone call on the fifth night, some things will be the same, but some things will be different. My father will have to be pushed in his wheelchair to the tall silver menorah. A grandson will guide his hand as he lights the wick in the oil cylinder and gently prod him as he haltingly recites the blessings.

And when the flames are kindled and illuminating the room, someone will say, "Zeide, let's sing *Maoz Tzur*."

My father will look momentarily perplexed and then he will furrow his brow in concentration, remembering a time that we know little about. Everyone will watch as he draws out the memory that is imprinted on his psyche and in a low, faltering voice, he will begin to sing.

They will let him sing alone for a few moments and then his children and grandchildren and great-grandchildren will add their voices, softly at first, but growing ever louder. When the final crescendo dies out and the last melody has been sung, there will be tears in my father's eyes. And he will smile.

— *Fay Kranz Greene*

Hanukkah possesses broad human significance and it is far more than a mere Jewish celebration. As a festival of liberty, it celebrates more than the independence of one people. It glorifies the right to freedom of all people.

— *Theodor Herzl Gaster*

I never knew that, according to Jewish law, women are required to refrain from all work and concentrate on the Hanukkah candles during the duration of their burning.

According to the *Laws of Hanukkah*, "… the miracle and salvation of Hanukkah was a result of the actions of Jewish women. Therefore, for at least a half hour after the flames of the menorah are kindled, women should not engage in any work."

Finally, a Jewish law I understand!

— *Nancy Rips*

3

who can retell?

A potpourri of Hanukkah memories away from home — From an RV Camp in California, the ice in Finland and even aboard Spaceship Hubble.

The Jew's home has never been his castle. Throughout the ages it has been something far higher—his sanctuary.

— *J.H. Hertz*

As a child, my dad recognized my interest in science and encouraged it. Both of my parents took me to planetariums and to "Tomorrowland," — the futuristic theme park at Disneyland. But I never thought I'd be celebrating Hanukkah in space, aboard the spaceship Hubble.

One of my first major experiences as an astronaut was seeing Tel Aviv and Jerusalem at night from the spacecraft. Watching the meteor enter the earth's atmosphere was like being in a fast-moving ping pong ball. It was an amazing experience.

I was a member of the first repair crew for the Hubble mission. It took two hours just to suit up and that was just the beginning. Repairing the telescope with power tools was meticulous work. It's a little like working on your car, but we were free floating in space, going from day to night every 90 minutes, looking back at the colored marble that is the earth. Our work was crucial because if something were to malfunction on the Hubble, it would not be able to send back to earth the images that have altered our knowledge of the universe. When we floated away from the Hubble, we were sorry to see it go.

When I realized the Hubble mission would occur during Hanukkah, I decided to carry along a few appropriate Jewish objects. An Israeli artisan presented me with a traveling silver miniature menorah and some dreidels. I wasn't planning to do anything public about Hanukkah because during Apollo 8 a big deal had been made about reading from the Bible in space and the astronauts had came under fire for this. "Wasn't there supposed to be a separation between government and religion?" the critics asked.

But when I had free time toward the end of the mission I decided to try spinning the dreidel. Because of gravity in space, it never stopped spinning. The top floated magically in the cabin, suspended in mid-air.

I was struck by the juxtaposition of the Jewish tradition, one of humanity's oldest, with space flight, one of humanity's newest. Our religion proved to be extremely portable as well as long lasting.

And what did my mom do while I was actually in space? She worried. That was her job.

— *Jeffrey A. Hoffman, Ph.D.*

Hanukkah in Israel is a much more subdued affair than is Christmas in the States. Christmas is the single most important holiday in American culture, whereas Hanukkah places a distant fourth in Israeli culture, behind Passover, Rosh Hashanah/Yom Kippur, and Sukkot. In fact, unless you have kids in school who get off for the week of Hanukkah while the rest of the country is officially at work, the holiday of Hanukkah might not be such a holiday at all. You might prefer to take a winter vacation at a time when all those screaming little kids will be back in school, plus your employer will be happy that you took up the slack while those with kids took a few days off during the holiday.

And so, what is most striking for an American Jew in Israel during December is not so much the experience of Hanukkah as a national holiday, but the absence of Christmas as a national holiday. It is quite a relief to live in a country where one is not bombarded by the theme of a holiday in which one takes no part.

Sometimes Hanukkah coincides with Christmas, sometimes it doesn't. This lack of contiguity matters a good deal to American Jews, but largely goes unnoticed in the Jewish

State. In America, when December 25th falls within one of the eight days of Hanukkah, Jews are in sync with their surrounding culture: They celebrate at the same time that the majority of Americans celebrate. In Israel, Christmas is not on the cultural radar for most Israeli Jews, and so whether or not it falls during Hanukkah hardly makes a ripple in an Israeli's consciousness.

Not observing Christmas in America is an important element in one's American Jewish identity. Part of what makes me a Jewish American is that I don't celebrate Christmas. It follows, therefore, that any time it is assumed that all Americans celebrate Christmas, I (to some extent) will be offended. Indeed, one is only mildly aware of the holiday in passing.

In Israel, Jews don't have to measure themselves against a different religious culture. Indeed, religious Zionism's dream was that in a country where Judaism is the majority culture, it can grow and thrive in ways unimaginable in the Diaspora. However, this dream was put on hold, in part because for the last four decades so much time and energy has gone into settling the territories, often in homogenous religious communities. In the wake of the disengagement from Gaza, one of the lessons that was learned by many religious people is if religious Zionism wants to reclaim its dream, it first must reconnect with the secular Israeli public.

Working in this vein, Rabbi Shlomo Riskin, a major spiritual leader of the national religious camp, founded a program called "Yachad," which means "together." Yachad places Jewish-renewal facilitators in community centers throughout Israel, connecting the secular Israeli public to their Jewish heritage on their own terms. A Hanukkah project developed two years ago by one of these Yachad facilitators was officially adopted this year by the Israel Association of Community Centers. The project is called "Ner Mehaber," meaning "The Candle That Connects." It unites families in a community from different ends of the social, cultural, or religious spectrum by pairing them for menorah candle lighting in one of their homes. The idea is not only that the project gives everyone the opportunity to celebrate and learn about the holiday of Hanukkah, but that it ultimately helps build stronger communities.

— *Teddy Weinberger*

I live in London, and when my children were small, the week before Hanukkah they would make a Hanukkah box. This was our variation on a Hanukkah bush. I would take them to the supermarket to pick out a cardboard box. We would then go and buy colored paper, sticky back plastic, silver foil, glitter, cotton wool, a few Christmas decorations, glue, scissors, and whatever else they fancied.

We would then spend a couple of nights cutting out and decorating each box. Each child had his or her own. This turned out to be something quite magical. We really did enjoy our "Walton moment." The boxes would then be filled with eight wrapped gifts from me, and any other presents they were given would also go into the Hanukkah box. Not all of the presents were expensive. Some were socks or pens. It was the whole experience of unwrapping a gift that they loved.

When we lit the menorah, they would go and pick a couple of gifts each night to open. It just added something special to the holiday. Now my children are grown up, and I'm sure they would enjoy making their special boxes, but they are very happy to just receive Hanukkah gelt.

I guess I will have to wait for the arrival of another special gift—grandchildren!

— *The Jewish Princess(aka Tracey Fine & Georgie Tarn)*

* * *

In Bulgaria, on the first night of Hanukkah, President Georgi Parvanov, is invited to light the *shamash* candle at Sofia's Central Synagogue. By tradition this candle is lit by a person who is respected in the Jewish community. After the service, a special celebration continues with a Hanukkah Night Party at the Jerusalem Hall of the Jewish Culture Center in Sofia.

— *Sofia News Agency*

* * *

Hanukkah's fried cuisine is just as popular here in France as it is in the U.S. We whip up dough balls *en friture* for our family.

— *Babette Keyser*

Hanukkah in modern-day Iran is only a wishful dream. Yet, when I was growing up during the Shah and the Islamic republic, Jews were able to practice their religion and study Hebrew. Under the Shah, you could be any Jew you wanted to be: Reform, Conservative, or Orthodox. You could have an Israeli flag. Now the Jews of Iran are under the laws of Islam.

I was born in Tehran in a modest home near Pahlave Street, a stone's throw from the marble Palace of Mohammad Rez Shah Pahlavi. I grew up in a large family with two brothers and four sisters. I attended a Muslim public elementary school and studied Judaism in evening classes.

We didn't have rabbis as teachers. The teaching was done by "learned Jews," who formed a committee in each town and would teach the children.

Once a year students would graduate from their Jewish classes, and the graduation always happened during Hanukkah. We had a large graduation. We would have a table set up in a big hall with a number of gifts: pens and pencils, albums, transistor radios, and tennis rackets.

The best students were called first so they had their first choice of the gifts. I was in the bottom of the line. I always wanted the transistor radio, but by the time I got to the table, there were just pens and pencils left. After the ceremony we would go to the largest Jewish high school to watch a Hanukkah play.

Now, in the United States, Hanukkah to me means the celebration of freedom - freedom of mind, thoughts, and ideas; freedom of social and economic practices; freedom of politics and choice. The holiday represents true democracy. The miracle of Hanukkah is as internal to me as it is external.

We are thankful for the miracles—the miracle of being free, of being part of a flourishing and freely practicing Jewish community, and of being able to practice *tikkun olam*, which means repairing the world.

— *Isaac Yomtovian*

finding a menorah in Ireland is a cinch, even though there are only 2,000 Jews out of a population of 4.4 million people. For some reason, thousands of rural Irish homes have unwittingly adopted this famous candelabrum to celebrate, of all things, Christmas. It's a Festival of Lights for sure, but somehow the Irish have taken it in a whole new direction.

During the 1990's, the Irish craze for menorahs took off. Probably some salesman with a hard neck or a thing for irony brought them to High Street, where they were instantly snapped up.

Driving west from Dublin to Galway in December, you can count menorahs by the hundreds, shining out from the polished windows of Irish living rooms. Some feature candles, some electric lights, but all seem designed to perplex their Jewish neighbors.

As President of the Progressive Jewish Congregation in Dublin, I'm not concerned. Mary McAleese, the President of Ireland, always puts a menorah in the window of the President's mansion, the *Aras an Uachtarain*, when

Hanukkah arrives. She lights an advent candle, as well.
The symbolism of dispelling darkness with light
transcends every faith and culture so I'm not concerned.

— *Malcolm Lewis*

* * *

We have Hanukkah celebrations on the ice in Finland. Our dreidel games are races played on the actual ice. The winner is the person who can keep the dreidel spinning on the ice for the longest time.

— *Hanna Kanter*

Hanukkah is a fairly new addition to the Indian Jewish tradition, but at New York's Indian Consulate, a group of Indian Jews throw a Hanukkah party every year. It's their attempt to bridge the gap between their culture and the majority culture of American Jews. Even though Jews have lived in India since the time of Antiochus, the villain of the Hanukkah story, Indian Jews began celebrating Hanukkah only about 200 years ago.

According to Romiel Daniel, President of the Indian Jewish Congregation of USA, "We hold the party in the Consulate so we can increase awareness of the fact that there are Jewish populations of different ethnicities here in this country. We do the regular Hanukkah rituals in a unique kind of chant. Then we eat fried Indian snacks. It makes us feel like we're back home in Bombay."

— *Marissa Brostoff*

Growing up in Buenos Aires in the 1950s and 1960s, I never saw a menorah. Many years later, after finishing my architecture studies, I began my career in New York and for the first time was living in a city where Jewish holidays are part of the cultural landscape. To my surprise, apartment windows, office buildings and stores all displayed menorahs. Even the Empire State Building is lit blue and white for the occasion. And my best friend made sure I received a little gift for every one of the eight nights of Hanukkah. I quickly learned that the holiday of Hanukkah existed, but I still wasn't sure of its meaning, nor the point of celebrating it.

Several years later my office sent me to Barcelona to work on a project. Even before my work was completed, I was determined to make this city my new home. After four years in Spain, I accepted an invitation to an evening Shabbat service. It was my very first Shabbat, but not the last as I soon participated in services every Friday evening, and eventually joined a new congregation, the first Reform synagogue in Spain.

Suddenly, the year was full of Jewish holidays replete with history, meaning, interpretations and traditions. I never knew when they would occur until there was an announcement in the Jewish community newsletter. Not accustomed to following the Hebrew calendar, I would inevitably miss a candle lighting or an important lecture in the community.

Unlike New York City, in Spain you still do not see anything obviously Jewish on the streets. One cannot find a Jewish business or a Jewish name on some sort of sign or even an indication on the doors of any of the active synagogues. Jews began returning to Spain about a century ago, but we are now less than 1 of 1,000 of the population. Though this may explain such absence from the public space, it puzzled me to observe that the same was true in the old Jewish quarter. This small neighborhood in the old part of town, known as *El Call*, is loaded with history. To preserve our Jewish story I started taking visitors on educational walks in this old Jewish quarter.

Some time ago in early December, when the sun had already set and I was not in a rush to return home, I decided to take a stroll on these same streets by myself. Cold weather did not stop me. I felt the need to try to capture what the spirit of the season may have been back then. How was Hanukkah celebrated in the Middle Ages, when Jews were living here? There is archaeological evidence of it, fragments of little clay oil lamps found in excavations. Did children love the holiday as they do today? Did they put Hanukkah lights in the windows? How did they keep the oil from spilling?

It did not take much to travel back in time and as I entered the *Carrer de la Font,* my mind started to wander. Here is where the well was, and right next to it are the remains of the arch leading to the narrow alley that ends at the *Sinagoga poca.* After a turn onto the *Carrer de la Volta* and then at the *Carrer de la Sinagoga Major,* I could see, even in the darkness, traces of tiny windows in some stone walls, remains from the 14th century.

Though I already knew the neighborhood like the palm of my hand, with the dim street light it was hard to find my way around. On my next left turn a doorway crowned with little colorful lights intrigued me. One, two, three . . . I counted. I counted again . . . four, five, six, seven. . . . There were eight lights over that door! In a neighborhood with no Jewish life for so long, was it possible that someone was still celebrating Hanukkah in *El Call*?

Approaching the door, I could see an old woman with gray hair pulled into a bun and a plaid apron with large pockets worn over her clothes. She was rearranging hundreds of items piled on the shelving and tables. For a second I thought that she was one of my Russian *bubbes*, and I almost ran inside to get my Hanukkah gift for the night.

But the embarrassment at my naiveté and the confusion it created in me made me anxious. I had to leave that neighborhood as fast as possible and move on without stopping or letting anything else distract me along the way.

I doubled my pace and soon reached the "real world," which happened to be the middle of the Christmas market. It was still comforting to know that year after year, these stalls had been set up in that same square in preparation for this holiday.

After that episode I have returned to *El Call* day after day, with visitors or by myself. When I turn that corner I always look for the doorway, hoping to see it in the light of day and explore what is beyond. But all I find is a rolled up shutter, which like many others in the neighborhood, had not been opened in a long time and was covered with graffiti.

To this day, I am not sure what I saw that night. Sometimes I wonder if, in my effort to reconnect to my Jewish heritage, it was merely a product of my imagination creating an event that I wish would have happened.

— Dominique Tomasov Blinder

* * *

Last year for the first time the Jewish community of Zagreb, Croatia, gathered for a public menorah lighting. The Mayor, Milan Bandic, commented, "I have a great merit that in this city, we can practice religion in freedom. In this city we can light the menorah without fear."

— Synagogue Bulletin

We celebrated Hanukkah in Antarctica. In December of 2004 we booked a dream trip to Antarctica on board the Explorer II, a luxurious small cruise ship converted from a former Russian icebreaker. Everything was planned. We both were very excited to be cruising to our sixth continent. However, after checking the calendar, we realized we would be gone the entire week of Hanukkah.

Being the experienced travelers that we are, we packed candles, a menorah, song sheets, piano music, and assorted decorations. On board ship we discovered many other Jewish shipmates, so a Hanukkah party was soon in the works. It was helpful that the Activities Director was Jewish, so he took charge of arranging the big celebration.

Word of the party soon traveled around the ship and even some non-Jewish cruise members expressed their desire to participate since they had never been to an authentic Hanukkah celebration.

The evening of the party arrived. We went early to set up the menorah and decorations in the ship's theatre. A piano was available for the music, and we anxiously awaited the guests' arrival. Soon the place was filled with Jews, closet Jews and non-Jews! Our Cruise Director outdid himself with the traditional holiday fare: Latkes with sour cream and applesauce, Hanukkah cookies, and plenty of wine for all.

So it was that in the middle of the icebergs and penguins of Antarctica, we sang the familiar songs, lit the candles and ate latkes.

Time purists note, we lit the candles while it was still daylight, as it does not actually get dark in Antarctica in December! For many days afterwards we heard many of our fellow travelers, Jew and non-Jew alike, tell us how much they enjoyed celebrating this holiday that commemorated religious freedom in such an unlikely location on earth.

— *Carole and Wayne Lainoff*

We're a synagogue on wheels. we celebrate Hanukkah in our RV. we're a whole Jewish congregation of RVers. we call ourselves CHAI, which means LIFE, but in this case stands for chavurat Yehudim, which means 'friendship of Jews.' it's a congregation on wheels, with no walls and the open sky for a roof.

It all began when we invited several Jewish RVers to our motor home. we met them at an RV convention in Indio, California. Everyone was delighted to know they were not the only Jews traveling in RV's. we reached out to more fellow travelers and our first service was held in 2004 at a Claremore, Oklahoma, campground. we had to have a designated "challah finder" to drive 60 miles roundtrip to purchase the bread. we arranged camp chairs in a circle and set up folding chairs for noshes and drinks. as in traditional congregations, we began collecting dues from the now 165 coaches, the family unit of the motor coach world.

although we are mostly a social group, we now have abbreviated services whenever we meet over the weekend. we've also had rallies during sukkot and pesach and even had two members become b'nai mitzvah.

our synagogue on wheels for wandering jews is wonderful. after we get together, we all head out in different directions to the next adventure, until we meet again.

— *Donna and Jay Blumenthal*

For many years, my wife and I traveled internationally in December during Hanukkah. We've been in Muslim and Hindu countries like Malaysia where they do not recognize Israel and do not grant Israeli citizens visas, even to visit.

On one trip we struggled with the question: Should we light Hanukkah candles in the windows of our hotel room? How do we explain to customs agents what a menorah is? What about the Hebrew prayer book? Will they throw us out? Find a reason to arrest us? Will the people in the next room wonder what we are singing and chanting? Will the fire alarm go off in the room when we have 6, 7, 8, 9, candles burning? What if the wax drips on the furniture?

We just did it, and none of our fears materialized. We are Jews. Jews light candles and sing songs on Hanukkah. Jews celebrate and so did we.

The only thing missing were some real good latkes!

— *Andy Greenberg*

4

menorahs can light up our worlds and ourselves

The lights of the menorah remind us of the lights that shine brightly within each one of us.

Kindle the taper like the steadfast star

Ablaze on evening's forehead o'er the earth,

And add each night a luster till afar

An eightfold splendor shine above

thy hearth.

— *Emma Lazarus*

The ritual of lighting the menorah is an act in publicizing one's belief in the constant availability of hope. As each generation passes this ancient custom on, parents are constantly teaching their children that the battle can be won, that darkness can be overcome. Hanukkah stands as a symbol of what is possible.

— *Ron Wolfson*

* * *

The message of Hanukkah is to kindle the first light: to care, to be concerned, and to be uplifting to others. In the end, a little bit of light has the power to drive away the darkness.

— *Rabbi Avi Weiss*

"What! No candles for the menorah?" we cried when our father came home empty-handed from *la bodega*, the grocery store. What are we going to do, *tate* (father)? How are we going to fulfill the obligation to kindle those dainty Hanukkah lights?

Back home in Cuba where I was born and came of age, World War II was raging on the European continent and therefore commodities were few and rationed. The sugar, coffee, and tobacco harvest were earmarked for export. Beef and lamb were scarce. Rice only accompanied a fish or chicken meal when available. Milk, coal for cooking, and bottled drinking water were delivered by a horse-drawn wagon to the homes, and we always prayed for the glass bottles. "Please, Father in Heaven, help the bottles come unbroken." Otherwise, we had to use a cloth, like a clean handkerchief, to sieve the milk through to make sure that no glass would be found in the liquid and be ingested, thereby creating an alarming and life-threatening situation.

My father, Reb Mendl, of blessed memory, was a prominent figure on the island. He was a rabbi, a *mohel*, a *shochet*, a teacher and a wonderful friend. He cared for the less fortunate, and he always convinced the more fortunate to give *tzedaka* to a multitude of endeavors. *Shabbos* at my father's and mother's, Senora Malka, house was frequented by many Jews and non-Jews. These were people who had abandoned Europe just before of the onslaught of the hated and murderous regime that devastated Europe and six million of our dearest and innocent Jewish brethren.

Shabbos morning we would be awakened and instructed to recite the *Birkhot Hashahar*, the morning prayers. We would then walk to the synagogue to partake in the *Shaharit* morning Torah reading, *D'var Torah* and *Musaf* service.

On the way home we would pass a Jewish baker with a heavenly array of goodies, neatly arranged in the see-through case and made before *Shabbos* to be enjoyed by the steady pre-paid clientele. We could not wait to come home and eat after our morning prayers. The *Kiddush* was chanted. We would wash our hands and recite the *Ha'motzi* as we sat down to eat gefilte fish made from fresh orange roughy, *cholent*, and desserts. Afterwards, *zmirot* (songs) were sung.

But the best part was yet to come: Our father's most welcome and sought-after treat for the family.

Although money was tight and provisions were rationed, he always found a way to scrape up a few pennies and purchase soft drinks. Coca-Cola, Pepsi-cola, Seven-Up and Orange-Crush were the favorites of the day. He would pour the different beverages into a big pitcher filled with ice, mix it and dole out the contents slowly into our six-ounce cup allowance that we would savor just like the manna provided in the desert to the traveling Jews.

"Oh! I have an idea," our father shouted. "After *Shabbos* I will gather the metal bottle covers, clean out their protective cork inserts, get a wad of cotton and create wicks. We will then place the wicks in the metal bottle covers, fill them with oil and kindle the Hanukkah Lights."

Hanukkah came and our father's plan was put into action. We recited the blessings and sang the festive melodies. And as I stood watching those beautiful little flames dance in the soft breeze, I wondered, "Did the corporate entourages of the different beverage companies have only profit for their efforts in mind or did they also have in mind the need to satisfy the religious requirements of some unknown practitioners of the Jewish faith?"

— *Rabbi Maximo Shechet*

My favorite menorah has always been the one my mother brought home from Israel. Resembling an ancient tree branch, it is made of olive wood with spaces for candles carved into it. For some reason, one year we lost the eighth candle holder. For years I tried to convince my kids that we only celebrated seven nights of Hanukkah, but they weren't buying it.

— *Nancy Rips*

* * *

Since Hanukkah falls near the winter solstice, it is especially good to light candles. All the nice meanings of bringing light to the world can be beautiful. But perhaps we are lighting up the world because we don't know how to light up our own lives.

— *Ralph Levy*

Several years ago, after taking up woodworking as a hobby, the thought occurred to me to make a large menorah and give it as a gift to the synagogue.

I wanted to make this giant menorah because I remember as a child always comparing the symbols and imagery of Christmas with that of Hanukkah. I was envious of my non-Jewish friends. Their symbols and imagery were all large: A big tree, piles of presents, a giant Santa, a huge sled, and even large reindeer, whereas the symbols of Hanukkah were all small. We had a few coins, a tiny dreidel, and a small menorah on the table. My family would gather around and light small candles and recite the blessings.

As I grew older, the back story of Hanukkah became important for me, and some of that childhood envy began to dissipate. I still had misgivings when I would see an assembly of people standing around a small menorah to recite the blessings and I felt sorry for the children in Talmud Torah who sat in the back of the class and had trouble seeing the menorah on the teacher's desk. And what of the people sitting in the back of the sanctuary, I wondered as I constructed my own menorah.

While I worked on my menorah, I thought it would only be a matter of scale. So I built a life-sized menorah out of walnut with a granite based cover. Happily, it was well received. People commented on its beauty. It was used in the main sanctuary and in the chapel for services during Hanukkah. It was also taken into classrooms for the kids to use. Teachers told me they loved it and so did the students. I was even invited to light the candles on the occasion of our synagogue's 75th anniversary.

I was so happy the menorah was well received that I decided to make another one. The second one was constructed out of cherry wood and has a large Star of David on the top. It was built about one year after the first one.

After the second menorah was finished and delivered, my wife and I arrived for *Kabbalat Shabbat* services. The rabbi stopped me and said he had just seen the beautiful second menorah and asked why I had undertaken such a project when the first one was so wonderful. My glib response was, "I'm trying to earn my way into heaven." The rabbi looked at me quizzically and replied, "Milton, I don't know if you can get there one menorah at a time."

— *Milton Katskee*

On Hanukkah there's a menorah. It looks like there are eight candles but there's actually nine, including the helper candle that lights all the other candles.

— *Daisy Friedman, age 8*

* * *

We all light our own menorahs at our family Hanukkah party. My father lights the one his parents gave him as a child. My uncle always brings his menorah that uses oil. My father-in-law kindles the menorah his grandmother gave him when he was eleven and escaping Nazi Germany. And then there are our children's choices.One has a basketball menorah and our daughter just received a Barbie one.We create true family memories when together we add light to the darkness of the world, even though each of our menorahs is different.

— *Jennifer Silver*

On the last night of Hanukkah in 1995, our long-standing synagogue faced a momentous change. The congregation gathered to vote and decide on the direction we should take. A decision had to be made. Should we stay a member of the Orthodox Union, with a member rabbi as its leader, which would mean new requirements for us of separate seating, and refraining from using the microphone on Shabbat and holidays? Or would it be better to abstain from Orthodox affiliation and look for a leader who would allow our congregation to remain as it had always been: a congregation with mixed seating that used a microphone on Shabbat?

As the meeting began, the tension in the air was palpable and the stage was set for decision making. It was not a surprise that the majority preferred to stay with the long-standing arrangement of mixed seating. As people began to discuss their opinions, it became evident that even though the majority of congregants did not want a seating change, there was a clear sentiment of devotion to the synagogue.

One of the elderly congregants, who had previously been opposed to any change, confidently walked down the aisle, took the microphone in his hand, and spoke. In his quiet but determined voice he explained, "If this is what it takes to save my synagogue, then I will do it." That was the defining moment. People suddenly put their individual wants aside and a consensus was reached without so much as a vote. Our synagogue would remain Orthodox. It was a remarkable, selfless moment where a majority allowed an organization to continue, regardless of personal preference.

After the meeting, the menorah was lit because it was the last day of Hanukkah. It stood proudly on the counter, not knowing the drama that had preceded its lighting. There it sat, quietly proclaiming:

"Here I am reminding you that rededication happens in every generation.

Here I am ready to be a symbol, just like the glowing candles on the menorah".

— *Donald Gerber*

During the first four nights of Hanukkah in 2008, menorahs literally lit up our world and ourselves. My family and I were on our first trip to Israel that winter.

The first candle: We landed in Chicago on our way to Israel. Around sundown, our rabbi, Aryeh Azriel, called us all together. "It's Hanukkah, come let us light the lights." I thought we would gather, chant the blessing, and sing a song or two, since we couldn't light candles. However, I was wrong. Rabbi Azriel pulled out his menorah, candles, and finally matches from his backpack. Everyone was amazed. "How did you get that past security?" I believe he said, "I have my ways."

That first night in Chicago, we celebrated Hanukkah together in our little corner of the airport and sang Hanukkah songs. No gifts were given, no latkes eaten, just being together with the blessings and the lights, anxiously waiting for the next night in Israel.

The trip overseas was long and no one got much sleep, but we were all so excited, it didn't matter. At 10:00 A.M. we landed in Rome. We were to have a small layover before departing for Tel Aviv. It wasn't long before we all heard that we were delayed and then grounded. Next we were told Alitalia went on strike and there would be no more flights out until the evening. After hours of red tape, we made plans to go see Rome. Why sit in an airport all day when we are in Rome? One of our travel mates acted as our guide. He had maps of tourist sites and found the train schedule and led us to the Coliseum, to the Trevi Fountain, and various other sites in the city. By dusk we all came back together for pizza, pasta, and gelato, then boarded our cabs for the airport and our flight to Israel.

The second candle: No planes would be flying until 10:00 P.M. Again, Rabbi Azriel, who had met a group of students who were also stranded, pulled out his menorah, candles and matches. Our small group was joined by the fifty-some youth and various others waiting for flights. We prayed and sang *Maoz Tzur* and felt grateful to have each other and our new friends to celebrate with us.

About midnight the youth group was able to board the only flight going to Israel that night. We waited until 1:30 a.m. for another possible flight, and then went to find the nearest hotel and a bed.

The third candle: We were back at the airport at 7:30 A.M. We went to the gate to board the plane. Again, no plane. Through at least two more hours of talking to everyone we could to hopefully get us on our way, we went off again to see Rome. This time we went to the Vatican. We were back as instructed at 7 P.M. to wait for a possible evening flight. Again, Rabbi Azriel came to me, "Come let's have Hanukkah." Our group started small, but now we were up to almost 60 participants from all over the airport who heard the singing and came to join us.

That night I met a mother and her daughter from Toronto. She told me, "We are just trying to get home after a wonderful stay in Israel. You don't know how much this celebration means to us, joining with other Jews from worlds away."

Finally, we left for Israel, at 2:30 that next morning.

The fourth candle: This time we were in Israel. I had the overwhelming feeling that we had finally come home. We were celebrating Hanukkah all together on the shores of the Kinneret, at the Sea of Galilee. It was the most special Hanukkah ever.

— *Tami Field*

I remember the ugly orange candles. When I was a child every year we had them for Hanukkah. It never changed. As a child it was difficult to understand why we couldn't have something prettier like blue or white. And the orange candles took forever to melt. I like all the colorful candles we have now.

— *Jan Schneiderman*

* * *

The commandment to light the Hanukkah lamp is an exceedingly precious one, and one should be particularly careful to fulfill it, in order to make known the miracle, and to offer additional praise to God for the wonders which he has brought to us.

— *Maimonides*

Think about the candles, the mitzvah of putting the menorah by the window so all can see. The window for me is the world. we can be a light to the nation.

— *Rabbi Aryeh Azriel*

These lights we kindle,

The miracles and the wonders and the victories

that our ancestors accomplished, in those days at this season, throughout all eight days of Hanukkah

these lights are sanctified.

— *Masechet Sofrim*

* * *

The world's largest menorah in the world was designed by Yaacov Agam. It is 32 ft. tall, 28 ft. wide, and weighs 4,000 pounds. It was unveiled on December 29, 2005, opposite Central Park in New York City.

— *Synagogue Bulletin*

5

eight nights a week

*For eight nights we celebrate Hanukkah
with parties, presents, and games.
Even a dreidel champion is crowned.*

We've had family Hanukkah parties for years. Our first "Friends and Kids" Hanukkah party was in December 1981. After that it became an annual tradition. We rotated hosts and homes among many friends.

I created our now "Famous Dreidel Cake", and we decorated cookies and dreidel bags. The kids made free-form dreidels and star sculptures and drew a large menorah. All the children played "Pin the Candle on the Menorah." From that day forward each family brought their own menorah to light, but the Dreidel Cake has been served at every Hanukkah gathering.

When it came to making latkes for the parties, we couldn't take the smell of the oil. We ended up renting our synagogue's kitchen so we could make enormously huge quantities. We had to schedule the cooking date so it would be the day before my mom's weekly hair appointment! And the minute we were through cooking, clothes immediately went into the washing machine.

It was a wonderful time of homemade projects and activities.

— *Cheryl Cooper*

Hanukkah calls for parties—latke parties, crafts parties, sing-a-long parties

In Seattle, kids have a "Hanukkah Pajama Jam." Over one thousand kids and parents come together at the Jewish Community Center to rock the house in their PJ's.

In Dobbs Ferry, New York, there's a Hanukkah Balloon Show. There's a Latke-Palooza at the Spertus Institute in Chicago, and a Hanukkah Kiddie Rock Concert in West Hartford, Connecticut.

At New York City's Jewish Museum, they feature a puppet show titled, "The Mystery of Hanukkah Harry." There's also a Hanukkah Sculpture Workshop and crazy melodies from "The Macaroons."

Hundreds of people meet at the Woodbury Ski area in Litchfield, Connecticut, every year to celebrate "Hanukkah on the Slopes" with live entertainment. There's candle-making, a menorah factory, and Hanukkah sand art. Judah Maccabee of old is also on hand to greet youngsters and their families.

Even the White House has a party. And just like everyone's family get together, something always goes wrong. Former President George W. Bush sent invitations with a Christmas tree on it, and President Barack Obama called it a holiday reception instead of saying it was specifically for Hanukkah.

— *Nancy Rips*

* * *

On hanukkah I get to be with my cousins and play games and sing songs.

— *Eleanor Dunning, age 8*

At our Hanukkah party, we asked everyone to bring a blank envelope with a one, five, ten, or twenty dollar bill in it. All the envelopes were placed in a basket.

The children and teenagers were invited to select three charities that could benefit from these donations. After much brainstorming and discussion, they came up with the Israeli Forrest Fire Fund, the Food Bank, and the Red Cross. Each charity name was put into a basket.

Then the game began. Each person received a Hanukkah question. When answered successfully (you could ask for a lifeline if needed), you picked an envelope and placed it in the charity basket of your choice.

Everyone participated, we all learned something new about Hanukkah, and we could do something for others at the same time.

Just like Hanukkah does each year, our game lit the spirits of all of our friends and family.

— Ann Goldstein

Although Hanukkah is not supposed to be about presents, each year my siblings and I looked forward to being able to open one gift per night from our parents. On the first night of Hanukkah my mother would place all of our gifts in the living room so we could choose which gift to open. It was important to have a gift opening strategy because Hanukkah normally fell while school was still in session, and every morning my friends would ask what I had received the prior night. Unlike my Christian friends who received big ticket items for Christmas, we would get a couple of nice gifts mixed in with a lot of practical gifts. There was nothing like opening a package of socks then going into school the next day and having my friends inquire as to what I had opened. Therefore, it was best to open soft items that had the potential to be undergarments or pajamas on the weekend with the hopes that on Monday my friends would talk about their weekend rather than ask about my presents. Despite the practical nature of the gifts, my non-Jewish friends were jealous that we received a present a night for eight nights, and I did nothing to change their perception.

— *Ellen Grishman*

On Hanukkah night, I often played Santa.

I'm also an amateur chef and like to entertain. One Hanukkah while preparing for a dinner party, setting tables, putting up decorations, placing chairs around the table, and making potato latkes, I was interrupted by the phone ringing. It was a friend who desperately needed someone of my measurements to play Santa, just for that night. Since she couldn't find anyone else, I agreed to visit four homes dressed as Santa.

At first I was reluctant. My place was here, preparing dinner. However, the distance around my waist, which I like to think of as a tribute to my culinary skills, made me a likely candidate as either Santa or a cook. How could I do this? I am Jewish, and whoever heard of a Jewish Santa? But on the other hand, Jews do sub on Christmas, at nursing homes and local hospitals, so non-Jewish staff members can enjoy their holiday. Was this so different? And I owed this friend a favor. And I hated to disappoint one particular little boy who had just lost a favorite uncle. So I buckled under the pressure and finished up what I was doing, hopped onto my sled and left.

The little boy Roy and his family had just returned from the funeral. They were so down that you could feel the sadness in the house. I asked Roy what he wanted from Santa. When he said he wanted his mother to smile again, it brought tears to my eyes. Roy left and returned from the kitchen, carrying a bag of oranges for Santa. I gave him his gifts, and as I was getting ready to leave, the Santa pants, which were too big even for me, fell to the floor, along with a few pillows. Even though I had my walking shorts on underneath, it was still so embarrassing, I couldn't get out of there and on my sled fast enough. However, the entire family, despite their recent bereavement, was laughing so hard; they said it was the most fun they'd had for the entire holiday season. As for me, notwithstanding the embarrassment, I was glad to have provided a lighthearted moment to a little boy and his family in the midst of their grief, and in the midst of my Hanukkah.

— *Stuart Stoler*

Congratulations! You have just purchased your first dreidel!

No, you didn't. You've never actually purchased a dreidel in your life, have you? You wouldn't even know where to go to get a hold of one. The toy store? The plastic dreidel deposits in Central America? The candy store? Actually, that last one is not so far off if you're in the market for one of those big hollow dreidels filled with nosh. But we all know that that's not really a dreidel.

Yet, you somehow have a mountain of dreidels at home, accumulated over the years from various schools, mid-winter birthday parties, etc. But none of these dreidels came with instructions. In fact, we at the Bureau of Instruction Manuals are even led to believe that you have no idea what to do with a dreidel, which is why we came up with:

DREIDELS FOR DUMMIES: The Instruction Manual

Do not swallow.

Now that we got #1 out of the way, we should also point out that THIS TOY IS NOT RECOMMENDED FOR CHILDREN UNDER THE AGE OF THREE, UNLESS

THEY ARE "WITH IT" ENOUGH TO BE ABLE TO READ THIS WARNING. Small children will try to swallow anything they can get their hands on, especially dreidels, which come in colors that are similar to many of the "candies" that have been approved for human consumption. Also, small children take forever to spin the dreidel on their turn.

ORIGINS: The dreidel originated during the time when many Jews hid away in caves to learn Torah until such time as the Greek soldiers showed up, which was when they hid their prayer books and pretended they were playing an innocent game of dreidel. "Oh!" exclaimed the guards, who were somewhat relieved. "This isn't a secret school! It is simply a bunch of grown men sitting around in a cave and playing with a top!"

Nowadays, most dreidels are handed out in Hebrew School, where the children practice spinning them until the Rabbi shows up, at which time they pretend to be learning.

OBJECT OF THE GAME: The object of the game is to win. But in case anyone asks, winning doesn't matter as long as you have fun. But there's only so much fun you can have with a game that doesn't require batteries.

MATERIALS NEEDED:

> 1 dreidel, or 1 dreidel per person, plus a pile of dreidels that everyone stays away from because they're "bad luck."

> A bunch of pennies, the exact amount depending on such factors as how many people are playing, how long the game is expected to take and who is providing the pennies. (Beans, nuts or Pokémon cards may also be used.)

> A hard, level playing surface, such as a dinette table, a hardwood floor or a tennis court.

> A pan of latkes sizzling in the background. This provides atmosphere in the form of spattering noises. If the game goes into overtime, it also provides atmosphere in the form of smoke.

> 1 pot.

PLAYERS: Anywhere from 2 players to 6.4 billion players, as long as you're willing to invite complete strangers off the street to come into your home and gamble. Just keep an eye on your pennies, as well as your children.

Along with everyone else, each game of dreidel must include:

> › 1 Show-Off : This is a person, usually male, who will make sure everyone notices, at each of his turns, that he is spinning the dreidel upside down on its handle.

> › 1 Dreidel-Dependent : This person will remind everyone over and over that he got the worst dreidel of the bunch and that, if anything bad happens, including the latkes exploding, it is entirely his dreidel's fault.

> › 1 Floor Guy : This person cannot spin a dreidel without having it fall violently onto the floor or, if you're already playing on the floor, through the hall and down the stairs. He or she will then pick up the dreidel, announce what letter it says and throw it back into the playing area in a way that leaves the other players doubting that he's even bothered to read the dreidel. This person usually wins.

> › 1 person who keeps announcing that next year he's going to bring in a weighted dreidel, so that he'd always get a "gimmel."

> › 1 person who actually has a weighted dreidel and doesn't realize it.

GAME PLAY: Game play begins when each player spins as

many dreidels as he or she can simultaneously and then tries to choose one to use throughout the game. Allow about one hour for this.

ACTUAL GAME PLAY: The first player spins the dreidel and waits for it to stop spinning. He then looks at it, frowns and says, "Okay, that was a practice spin." Then he spins it again. When the dreidel finally lands on its side, the player follows the instructions corresponding to the letter shown on the dreidel:

› NUN: The player does nothing. He simply sits there and stares in the general direction of his dreidel until the next player gets tired of waiting and spins his own dreidel.

› GIMMEL: The player can do a short victory dance, and then he can take all of the pennies from the pot in the middle of the playing area. Then he can put one or two back into the pot, along with everyone else, because otherwise there's no real point in the next guy going. Or, if you want a really short game, the game is over when someone gets a "gimmel," and cheating is allowed.

› HEY: The player takes half of the pot. If there are an odd amount of pennies in the pot, a major argument ensues and the game is basically over.

> SHIN: The player puts some of his pennies back into the pot and then switches to another dreidel.

Game play then continues in the order in which the players are sitting, because otherwise it gets confusing.

THE WINNER: The winner is the player who is left with the most pennies at the end of the game. He gets to keep his pennies.

THE LOSER: The loser is the guy who supplied the pennies in the first place.

ENDGAME: The game ends when it is time to put out the latkes.

— *Mordechai Schmutter*

* * *

My mom and dad hide our presents. When we look for them on Hanukkah, they tell us if we're cold or hot.

— *Leo Kohll, age 6*

The dreidel has served as both a children's toy and a religious symbol for centuries of Hanukkah celebrations. It's marked with the Hebrew letters that stand for "a great miracle happened there." Artist and Jewish scholar Marsha Plafkin Hurwitz's version of the four-sided top is more than child's play, though. It's also a conceptual sculpture, disability aid, and sensitivity tool.

She fashioned a metal dreidel featuring raised Braille bumps, called "The Breidel." It's in the collection of the National Museum of American Jewish History in Philadelphia. Now it's finding fans among disability-rights advocates.

— *Nicole Neroulias*

* * *

What do I like best about Hanukkah? Opening presents.

— *Aiden Meyerson, age 4*

On the first night of Hanukkah, take your children with you when you volunteer to serve meals at the local homeless shelter. Light one candle to illuminate their darkness.

On the second night of Hanukkah, take your children to the local hospital, and show them how to give a teddy bear or a doll to one of the young patients. Light one candle to illuminate their darkness.

On the third night of Hanukkah, you and your children should take an old coat or an old blanket downtown and give it to a homeless person who is cold. Light one candle to illuminate their darkness.

On the fourth night of Hanukkah, you and your children should take a pair of socks downtown and give it to the same homeless person you met the previous night. Light one candle to illuminate their darkness.

On the fifth night of Hanukkah, take your children to visit some of the folks living at the local retirement home. Sing a few songs, tell a few stories, hold a few hands, and comfort them in their loneliness—and listen to their wisdom. Light one candle to illuminate their darkness.

On the sixth night of Hanukkah, take your children to the local blood bank, and let them watch as you donate a pint of blood, as you give the gift of life. Light one candle to illuminate the darkness.

On the seventh night of Hanukkah, take your children to play with the young ones at the local women's shelter. Light one candle to illuminate their darkness.

On the eighth night of Hanukkah, take your children to an elderly neighbor's house and cook, straighten up, vacuum, scrub the bathtub and the toilets, clean the oven. Light one candle to illuminate the darkness.

On every night of Hanukkah, invite friends and neighbors, teachers and classmates, relatives and business associates into your house. Make your home a place of learning and light, of high purpose and deep spirit. Hold your children, hug them tight, and tell them how much you love them. Give your children the gift that will last a lifetime—the gift of compassion, of sweetness, of humanity, of soul. Light one candle to illuminate the darkness.

— *Wayne Dosick*

It's the first night of Hanukkah, and only one person can take home the crystal dreidel trophy. The Major League Dreidel championship is on.

The legendary players arrive early at a bar on the Lower East Side of Manhattan. With nicknames like "Debbie Does Dreidel" and "Jewbacca," this is no longer a sport for children.

Pamela "Pamskee" Goldman, last year's champion, comes in with a target painted on her spinning wrist. Everyone wants to beat her world record spin: 17.8 seconds.

The "knishioner" of Major League Dreidel, Eric Pavony, points out that this is not your rabbi's dreidel. In the traditional Hanukkah game, the spins are left up to chance, and only luck can win you the chocolate coins known as gelt.

But Pavony came up with something a little more challenging: Spinners compete on how long their dreidel spins on increasingly smaller surfaces. On the "Spinagogue," as they call it, only skill can bring home the gelt.

Everyone has a technique. Tasmanian Dreidel spins with his whole body. Dre-idol has covered his fingers with wax and plans to spin the top upside down. But Pamskee sets the standard. She uses only the barest of movement with her fingertips to get her world record spins.

The night starts with 64 competitors set up in brackets. It's like the NCAA, Pavony says, except more Jewish.

By almost midnight, there are only two left: Pamskee and the runner-up from last year's competition, the man known as Virtual Dreidel. As the crowd pulls in, it starts chanting "Spin, spin, spin, spin."

Virtual Dreidel removes his scarf, looks across the table at Pamskee and nails a perfect spin to the center with a time of 15.4 seconds. He carries the dreidel over to her. She flubs the first spin then recovers with a beauty. Everyone looks to the judge who calls out her time: 12.1 seconds. There is a new dreidel champion.

Holding the trophy aloft, Virtual Dreidel reveals his real name: Howard Pavony. He is Eric Pavony's father. But there's no nepotism, he swears. The stopwatch doesn't lie.

Howard Pavony says his secret to a long, long dreidel spin is to remain calm, and not show emotion. It's like the holiday of Hanukkah itself, he says: "Just as the oil in the temple burned for eight days, so, too, a great dreidel player has patience and spirit."

Unfortunately for the champion basking in glory, Major League Dreidel has the shortest season of any professional sport. It's over and forgotten by the time that last Hanukkah candle is lit. But Eric Pavony would like to see it go a little longer.

— *Robert Smith*

* * *

Last year for the first time ever, our Hanukkah party took place in two cities at the same time: San Diego and Phoenix. We Skyped! It was so much fun. We got set up in Phoenix, two grandparents, a daughter and son-in-law (who knew how to make it work), three grandchildren, and a dog. Our other children were in San Diego. We sang the blessings together, lit the menorahs simultaneously, and heard all of the children in both cities sing, "I Have a Little Dreidel." Skype is wonderful. We're waiting for smell-a-vision, so we can smell the latkes in the other city!

— *Marlene Epstein*

6

DOES DECEMBER HAVE TO SPELL DILEMMA?

Hanukkah is not the same as Christmas, although they both occur during the same season, and that makes it a challenge for many families.

By a total accident of timing,
the minor holiday
of hanukkah falls close on
the calendar to a great holy
day of the christian faith.
This coincidence has all but
created a new hanukkah.

— *Herman Wouk*

Every December, our society is consumed with the Number One commercial extravaganza: The Christmas season.

Many well-meaning people assume that since Jews do not celebrate Christmas, we must feel deprived. Others simply do not know anything about Judaism, Jewish values or Jewish holidays and figure that Jews need something big to go along with Christmas.

Inevitably, Hanukkah becomes the Jewish Christmas since it happens to fall around the same time of the year. Big mistake. Hanukkah is not a Jewish version of Christmas. It is not the Jewish response to Christmas; it has nothing whatsoever to do with Christmas.

Christmas is one of the two most important Christian holidays. It is when Christians believe that the son of God, the Messiah, was born. It is a celebratory holiday of great religious significance. Gift-giving became a part of the tradition from the same sources that led us to give gifts on birthdays. All of the Christmas traditions and symbols have religious and social meanings. (Despite what the U.S. Supreme Court said a few years ago, there are no "secular" Christmas symbols. Christmas is meaningful to Christians, and saying

Christmas symbols have taken on a secular meaning is completely inappropriate. As Jews, we would certainly object to anyone saying our symbols are not "religious.")

Hanukkah, on the other hand, is not a really big holiday. It commemorates a military victory over oppressors a few hundred years Before the Common Era (B.C.E.).

It is not our most important holiday, or even on the list of our top five. The top five would be Rosh Hashanah, Yom Kippur, Passover, Shavuot, and Sukkot.

Hanukkah is not a Jewish Christmas. Christians celebrate the birth of their God—we celebrate the military victory over the Greeks, a winning battle in a lost war. The holidays are not even in the same ballpark. To equate them misleads people into thinking there is more significance to Hanukkah.

If we make a minor holiday with little religious meaning our most significant then what does it mean in terms of our understanding of ourselves, our religious values and ethics, and religious observance?

I believe Jews should not get involved in Christmas. If there are public displays of Christian symbols, let them be there.

We are a minority in this country and this holiday is not ours. When you live in a culture in which you are not in the majority, you have to expect that there will be some things you just can't participate in.

"Holiday" events do nothing for Jews but make us look like a poor little people who have nothing better than dreidels to talk about. Do the lyrics of "I Had a Little Dreidel" really compare with the majesty and significance of "Silent Night?"

It's inauthentic to put the two holidays into some kind of juxtaposition, which is what inevitably happens in "holiday" programs, which secularize a Christian holiday and distort a Jewish one.

The Jewish calendar is rich in celebrations, including Hanukkah. But when Hanukkah is the only expression of a person's Jewishness or Jewish awareness, it's vapid and inauthentic. The answer to Christmas is not Hanukkah. The answer is all of our holidays and special observances. It's our job to bring that awareness to the well-meaning people who simply don't know better.

— *Rabbi H. Rafael Goldstein*

Slam, pound, knead. Slam, pound, knead. Roll, roll, roll.

It was fall. December was coming. We were newly married, just a couple of years. Roll, roll, roll.

I had made a drawing on construction paper, a drawing of a tree, with a sunset behind it. With eight, no, nine branches, a taller one in the middle. As an art teacher, I had knowledge and enthusiasm and an art room full of space and supplies.

I placed the drawing over the rolled-out clay. I used a pointed clay tool, like a pin on a stick, to draw around the tree design onto the clay. I took a clay knife and cut around the paper drawing to establish the outline of the tree in the clay. I pulled off the outer scraps of clay and saved them. I poked the pointed clay tool through the paper at particular points of my drawing that was still on top of the clay. Then I could transfer the drawing more accurately onto the clay.

My husband and I were married in June, wed by my minister and a "Rabbi for Hire," a rabbi willing to perform an interfaith marriage in 1973. The ceremony blended our faith traditions openly and respectfully. We were optimistic that our marriage would flourish, and our love would bridge our religious differences. December challenged us.

Off came the paper. I used the point guides to begin drawing on the clay itself. I drew the tree, with the nine branches, the ground beneath it, and the sunset behind it. I carved a little into the clay, to separate the tree from the background, and to give it some depth of a relief to make it more interesting. I drew in lines for the bark on the tree, complete with knotholes and roots, which had grass growing over them as they entered the ground.

I took the cut-away clay scraps and rolled them thinner. I cut little rectangles for these scraps and rolled them over my finger, and then a smaller clay tool to make little cylinders. I scored the seams of the cylinders with crosshatch lines into the clay. I scored the top of the branches. One branch at a time, I painted on slip, a mixture of clay with water, onto each tree branch and onto the cylinders. One by one I lightly pressed the cylinders onto each branch. They would hold the candles.

Finished.

My husband was in Medical School. I was teaching art in the local elementary/middle school. I checked my tree regularly until it dried. I put it into the kiln and fired it. The gray clay turned white and hard.

I did not know what to do for my husband for Hanukkah, and money was not so available. I know that my menorah "Tree of Life" could serve as an example of slab clay work for the classes I taught in school. And it would be a lovely surprise for my husband.

I took out my watercolors and painted on the white kiln-fired clay. The grass below the tree I painted in greens, the sunset behind the tree in yellows and oranges, the bark of the tree I painted as a rainbow of colors. I turned the tree over and painted in blue, 'Happy Hanukkah, Howie! Love, Laura-Lee, the Bee." (Those were our nicknames for each other then -and now -37 years later.) When I was satisfied, and the paint was dry, I sprayed the clay tree with a clear varnish to protect the colors.

I loved Christmas. We had Christmas in our apartment with a live tree full of lights. It filled too much space. I really wanted to share in my husband's tradition and celebrate Hanukkah with all the love I felt for him. I had decided to make for him another kind of tree, a "Tree of Life," as a menorah. This, as a gift to him, would show my desire to share our holidays.

It looked great and I was so excited to give it to him. Once I did, he was thrilled. We wanted to use that menorah. But it was a flat tree that did not stand. I had some scrap pieces of wood from another art project. I glued three onto the back of the tree with a picture hanger nailed into one in the center of gravity of the back. We could then hang our menorah on the wall, put our candles in it and actually light them. The wood held the menorah a little away from the wall, so candles could be lit safely.

We used that menorah for years.

The only problem was smoke came off the candles. Every year the wall where the menorah hung got sooty black from smoke. We knew Hanukkah was over when we took the menorah down to roll on paint over the blackened wall.

Roll, roll, roll.

— *Laura-Lee Needelman*

My earliest memories of Hanukkah are similar to those I've heard of first Christmases: Anticipation, aching desire for presents, joy at receiving them, disappointment at not getting what I wanted or because the present wasn't half as cool in real life as it was in my imagination or on television, and festive food.

Hanukkah is one of many Jewish holidays I've heard described collectively as "Someone tried to kill us. They couldn't. Let's eat." It's not even one of the most important holidays. But it is unique because its position in the calendar puts it in line for comparison with the biggest, most commercial holiday in the Christian year. As a result, many, perhaps most, American Jews suffer Christmas envy.

When I was a kid, it didn't bother me much. My parents noted that we got presents for eight days, compared with the one day that the Christians had. (The full twelve days of Christmas were fortunately not commonly celebrated among our suburban New York neighbors.) My relatives went out of their way to make the holiday fun and exciting.

Though we never had a tree or electric lights, my grandmother would often take my sister, Kim, and me to New York City to view the Rockefeller Center tree and the intricately decorated store windows. Each year, when we were young, my mom took us to the Nutcracker ballet at Lincoln Center. On the way home at night, we'd count the lights and see how many decorated buildings we could spot.

I remember distinctly the year I realized that the tree in the ballet didn't really grow inexplicably larger but simply emerged from a hole in the stage. Perhaps it was then that holiday magic, for me, went into decline. I was probably around eleven.

As I grew up, I began to wonder about the meaning of Hanukkah. Christmas held numerous lessons about peace and love and giving, but Hanukkah began to seem almost militaristic. It celebrated victory in battle, and the main miracle—one day's worth of oil keeping the Temple's menorah lit for eight days—seemed pretty pale in comparison with a virgin birth marked by signs from the heavens. I felt guilty about my misgivings and couldn't, like so many secular or mixed-marriage Jews, decide to celebrate the idea of Christmas with a tree or other symbols. It felt wrong.

When I left home for college, my religious life itself pretty much ceased. I had been through a period of spiritual seeking with psychedelic drugs and an exploration of Buddhism, but I remained confused and questioning and unsure about my Judaism. I came home for the holidays, but it felt strange and perfunctory. My parents divorced, and celebrations became strained reminders of the split. Rather than anticipation, I began to feel dread. All the cards and trees and commercials with perfect families began to mock me and make me feel as though I was alone in my ambivalence.

— *Maia Szalavitz*

* * *

Having been raised Methodist as a child I always thought that Hanukkah was something like Christmas. After all, both were celebrated in December and everyone got presents. I certainly didn't understand the significance of the differences and that they had absolutely no relationship to each other. I've also since found out that some Jewish families, like some Christians, have lost sight of what their holiday really means—so much more than just presents.

My first Hanukkah, without explanation, didn't make a whole lot of sense to me. Since marrying my wife, Marti, and after twenty-plus years of celebrating Hanukkah and understanding its meaning, it not only makes a lot of sense, but also makes me realize how unfortunate it is that more Christians don't understand and that many Jews forget.

The holiday took on special meaning for me when we introduced three of our Catholic Atherton grandchildren to the Hanukkah celebration, complete with the telling and retelling of the Hanukkah story, blessings and songs, latkes with applesauce, low stakes dreidel games—and THEN the presents. The first, at about age eight, found it so fascinating that she wanted to start her own menorah collection! Now eighteen, she continues to bring them all and light up our home at each year's Hanukkah celebration. Out of this experience, understanding of the meaning of Hanukkah spread beyond our family to our granddaughters' Catholic grade school, where they invited Marti to come share the Hanukkah story as they lit candles, crafted menorahs, and took home their very own dreidels.

During the time of silent prayer at Friday evening's Kabbalat Shabbat services, I am drawn to the reading entitled, "No Religion Is an Island." *There is no monopoly on holiness,* it reads, *we share the kinship of humanity, the capacity for compassion.* For me, this prayer represents the meaning of Hanukkah even beyond religious freedom. Though we may be *diverse in our devotion and commitment,* Hanukkah also teaches us that it is incumbent upon us not just to accept and tolerate, but to understand and embrace the diversity that ultimately enriches our world. *Let mutual concern replace remnants of mutual contempt,* we pray, *as we share the precarious position of being human. Let us not be guided by ignorance or disdain. Let lives of holiness illumine all our paths.*

I've learned a lot since that first Hanukkah. It's about so much more than presents. And it does, indeed, make a lot of sense.

— *John Atherton*

I'm a Jew from New York, but I wasn't Jewish till I moved to the Midwest.

My mother and father were both raised Jewish in Rochester, New York. They dated, married, had me, followed by my brother, and divorced three years later. I was told we had a Jewish home. We celebrated Hanukkah and continued to do so after my parents separated, for another four years. Then my mother met my stepfather, and he put an end to everything Jewish. So there went Hanukkah and my Jewish identity.

My husband is from Newton, Massachusetts. He was raised Catholic, but since Newton is a town with a lot of Jewish people, he was more comfortable with Jewish customs than I was.

When we were new parents and the holidays arrived, we put up a Christmas tree. I can't remember if we had a menorah. We were living in Hanover, New Hampshire. I wasn't close with my family, and I thought we would do what my husband wanted. I told him that our children would never be baptized, I knew that much, but I had done Christmas and was familiar with the trimmings. So it was fine.

Then we moved to the Midwest. We joined a Temple and enrolled our children in religious school but we kept doing Christmas. We became more involved. We volunteered. My husband made friends and felt like a real member of the tribe, but we kept doing Christmas. I did all of the decorating, the buying and the wrapping. I did it, I said, for my husband, but I guess it's just the way our Jewish home evolved. Out of Christmas came Hanukkah. Out of my wonderful new community and my Catholic husband's acceptance of who I was, came our Jewishness. My husband wanted to have a family with traditions. Now we have two.

— *Hillary Fletcher*

We celebrate Hanukkah and Christmas equally and respectfully in our home. We have a Hanukkah room and a Christmas room, and it's in each designated room that we celebrate each holiday. The dining room is neutral and switches out depending on which dinner we're enjoying. Different tablecloths, napkins, centerpieces, and food represent our annual Hanukkah and Christmas dinners. The upstairs bedrooms and the basement recreation room have always remained undecorated for the holidays. Our breathing space.

One year we mushed everything together through the main floor of our house. But we didn't like that, and we went back to different rooms for each.

— *Sharon Comisar-Langdon*

My grandmother loved being Jewish, but I think it was her greatest regret in life not to be able to celebrate Christmas. It would have been her ideal holiday: Family, food, an unlimited amount of junk you can buy. She more than made up for it when it was her night to host Hanukkah at her house. Instead of a Christmas tree, we had the Hanukkah pool table; sometimes the gifts were piled six feet high. A person standing on one side couldn't see who was on the other. Some years, we had to use the stepladder from the garage to reach the presents at the top. My parents called it "the Festival of Greed," which wasn't nice. Apt, maybe, but not nice.

One year I remember that Grandma was really excited. When we got to the door she told us she'd found all this new Hanukkah stuff at the store that looked totally different than anything she'd ever seen before. She was really proud. She said it had the menorah and everything, but the colors were all different and it was all so beautiful. We walked upstairs into the dining room, where she had really gone crazy: Tablecloth, napkins, paper plates, streamers. It was different colors all right; everything was green, red, yellow, and black. My mother looked at the family lighting candles on one of the plates and said, 'If those are Jews, they must be Ethiopian Jews." Grandma had festooned the whole house with Kwanzaa decorations. I guess the Kinara, the thing with the candles in it, tripped her up. It's not so different, really, when you think about it.

— *Rachel Shukert*

* * *

One winter, my daughter came home from college and shared the results of a dorm "bull session." Trying to figure out why she hadn't turned to drinking, drugs, or carefree sex as had a number of those with whom she grew up, she had only one answer. "Hanukkah." Her reasoning? "When we had to celebrate Hanukkah while everyone else celebrated Christmas, I learned that it was OK to be different. I didn't have to do everything that everyone else did."

— *Patti Goldin*

Growing up, I never understood why Jewish kids would go crazy for a five-foot tinseled tree or long for the bluish glow of a Hanukkah bush.

We had our own dramatic rituals in the little town of Williamsport, Pennsylvania, population 50,000. Every Hanukkah a small committee, including the Rabbi, made the rounds to decorate houses for a friendly competition.

An old photograph rekindled my memory of this annual event, sponsored by our Conservative Synagogue. I see an awkward, stringy-haired girl with pointed glasses, me standing on one side of a homemade diorama and a shorter curly-haired girl (my sister), positioned on the opposite end. Inside the constructed scene, Maccabees sported their swords and gazed across the way to a papier maché menorah. In between are stony hills and the occasional tree. After scrutinizing the diorama, the committee took notes, commenting on the blue and white streamers overhead, ate a few dreidel cookies, and headed off for the next house. One family would win a prize for the best decorations.

It was a strange case of Jewish identity.

— *Joan Latchaw*

I guess the biggest thing was sharing the Holiday Seasons so we would celebrate the Hanukkah Season with our friends celebrating Christmas. They thought the menorah and eight nights of gifts were cool!

— *Lloyd E. Roistein*

* * *

One night during Hanukkah, we were at our daughter and son-in-law's house for dinner in Connecticut. They are an ecumenical family. There was a Christmas tree in the background and a menorah on the dining room table. Our daughter passed around the *shamash* so everyone could have a turn lighting the menorah. When it was our four-year-old grandson's time to hold the candle, he piped up with, "Where are the Kwanzaa candles"?

— *Bob Kully*

My mother is Jewish, but converted to Catholicism as a young woman. She raised my sister, brother and me in the Catholic Church with an understanding of our Jewish heritage, celebrating Hanukkah every year. We like to call ourselves Cashews (Catholic Jews).

One of my clearest memories of my childhood is Hanukkah, the Festival of Lights, probably because I enjoyed it more than Christmas. My mother had a Hanukkah Open House every year. We invited all our friends, regardless of their personal beliefs or religions. We would light the menorah at sundown, saying the prayers in both Hebrew (from a card with the phonetic spellings) and English. We had a huge pot of matzah ball soup, constantly dwindling stacks of latkes, a "fruits of Israel" platter, and Israeli donuts. The donuts were the biggest hit, those little fried balls of dough rolled in powdered sugar. Of course, we had wine, coffee, tea, and some apple cider for the kids. I loved helping Mom in the kitchen as she would often put me in charge of the matzah balls. I make a mean matzah ball. That was Hanukkah for me: The friends, family, and relaxation of that evening.

Christmas was different. Everyone worried about shopping for gifts, and we crammed too many people into our little house for Christmas dinner. It's one thing to have people coming and going all evening, but something else entirely to fit them all around our dining room table. Christmas was hectic and stressful.

For me, Hanukkah has always been a celebration of family and friends. Hanukkah is a time to sit and relax, to stare at the candle flames and contemplate whatever is on your mind. Hanukkah does not have the usual stress and hustle of the "holiday season." I have always tried to celebrate Hanukkah in my home, even if I miss lighting the candles a few nights. My husband and I will turn off the lights and just enjoy the glow of the menorah.

Recently, my husband, a non-Jew, and I have started embracing more of my Jewish heritage. We have studied and started celebrating the High Holy Days, which has just added to the meaning of Hanukkah for me. It reminds me of the history of my people, but also of my future. I am proud to be part of a people that has survived such hardship for so long.

This year, we will continue my mother's tradition of the Hanukkah Open House, inviting our friends for a fun, yet educational evening of food and light. We will answer any questions our friends have and just enjoy their company. We will say the prayers and light the candles. We will remember the past and hope for the future.

— *Charla E. Welch*

* * *

When I became engaged to a Jewish woman, she informed me that I had to give her eight big presents for Hanukkah, one each night. It took a while till I realized she was joking.

— *David Wilson*

* * *

I married two Catholic girls. They both insisted on having a Christmas tree every year. I agreed as long as they put a bagel on top.

— *Jeff Schrager*

We're an interfaith family, and we celebrate both Hanukkah and Christmas. For us that means hanging Christmas lights and lighting Hanukkah candles. We have an annual Hanukkah party with dreidels and latkes, but we also decorate a tree and bake cookies for Christmas. We want to be respectful of each tradition. And we try to help our kids connect the similarities.

The biggest issue for us is helping our two sons understand the meaning of both holidays. They love the fact that they get presents for both Hanukkah and Christmas, but we want to show them it's about more.

Some interfaith families blend both holidays together. We make a point to show that they are distinct and different.

— *Laura Wiseman*

Hanukkah celebrates
victory over oppression and
asserts values of freedom.
It speaks of the deepest
of human values,
not just Jewish ones.

— *Daniel Libeskind*

Shhhhh. Keep this to yourself.

We had a Christmas tree every year. Just as I wrote that, I could hear my mother pleading, "Oh, Nancy, don't tell that story."

Here's what happened. I loved the idea of Christmas. The colors. The activities. The gaiety. Who wouldn't? And I always wanted a tree.

Every year on December 24, late in the day, my dad and I would go to the corner Safeway grocery store and purchase the cheapest, leftover, most straggly tree there was. To my seven-year-old eyes, it was fabulous. We brought it home, and I zoomed up to the attic to bring down the decorations.

I can still hear my mom trilling, okay, shrieking, "Leo, do you have to? We're Jewish. What are we teaching our kids?"

He would answer, "Frances, we're teaching them that a tree is just a tree to be enjoyed. They know who they are; they're Jewish. We have Shabbat dinner every week. We attend services as a family. We observe all the holidays. Don't worry, they're Jewish. This is just fun. Exciting."

My dad was fun. Exciting. And those annual trees didn't make any of us less Jewish.

Shhhhh. Keep this to yourself. Even though my mom's been gone for 44 years, I can hear the shrieking in my ears.

— *Nancy Rips*

7

MY FAIR LATKES

Who wouldn't love a holiday where you're supposed to eat fried foods every night?

At hanukkah time, there's a whole lotta latkes going on. It's the one holiday that features oily food as a remembrance of the miracle of the Maccabees and the oil lasting so long. There are classic latkes made out of potatoes, but there are also zucchini latkes, Hatch green chili latkes, apple rum latkes, chocolate chip latkes, sweet potato, cottage cheese, and it had to happen—low fat latkes made with egg whites. I'll pass on those. I want the real thing—potatoes, oil, and salt. Cue the cardiologists.

— *Nancy Rips*

Hockey puck, slider, spud muffin, grease sponge, glue glob. Oh the shame of a latke gone wrong. Heaven forbid the guests at your Hanukkah party would have to digest a latke that merits such insult.

When it comes to latkes I wear the apron in my family. I'll make a latke worth ridiculing over my dead spatula.

What's a perfect latke? Golden brown on the outside, crispy around the edges, no thicker than $1.50 in quarters, and neither lumpy nor gooey nor crumbly. More sweet than salty, more chewy than doughy, moist not arid, limpid not limp.

A great latke never hides behind applesauce or sour cream; it invites them over for dinner. It tangos with brisket, plays footsie with green beans. It has your guests beg for more. A really great latke has enough oil to consecrate the Temple, produces enough heartburn to last only one day, but leaves a taste in your mouth for eight. A divine latke is a great miracle, and has the face of Moses fried on it.

What follows is my recipe for latkes that, given enough oil, shine.

WHAT YOU NEED:

› About 10 red or white potatoes (a couple of pounds)

› About 1 big sweet potato

› 1-2 carrots

› 1 huge onion (two smaller onions, if they're friends)

› 2 cloves of garlic (or the whole bulb, if you don't want friends)

› 3 tsp. curry powder

› 1 tsp. paprika

› 1 tsp. cumin

› 1 tsp. salt

› 2 tsp. baking powder

› 1 tsp. baking soda

› About 3 eggs

› About 1-2 cups matzah meal (the stuff left over from Passover if it isn't moldy)

› A dash of this, a pinch of that (use your imagination, think parsley)

> Olive oil. Not butter, not canola oil, not peanut oil. Where do you think Jews come from, Alaska? Do not cook with Pam (unless you're married), this is Hanukkah!

WHAT TO HAVE:
> Food processor

> Big stainless steel mixing bowl

> Big colander (but don't strain yourself)

> Wooden mixing spoon chewed at the end by the beaters of your mixer not your dog

> Iron skillet or griddle. (Drop that aluminum pan! You'll cook with IRON, you hear? Did you say Teflon? Drop down 'n gimme 20!)

> Big metal serving spoon

> Metal spatula

> Paper towels

> Baking sheet

WHAT TO DO:
> Wash and peel the potatoes, carrots, sweet potato, and

anything else that might have come into contact with fertilizer, chemicals, or vermin.

› Quarter the onions and remove the skin.

› Smash the side of the garlic clove(s) with the edge of a knife. The skin will come off easily. Be careful. So will your finger.

› Now you're going to use your food processor carefully. Stay focused. You need a light touch for that "on" button, like a cop in a hostage situation. You want to knock off the bad guy without killing the hostage. That's how you're going to blend the potatoes, carrots, sweet potato, onion and garlic. You do not want to chop them, and you do not want to puree them. You want to do something in between.

› Take this mixture from the food processor and put it in the colander. Get out the excess liquid. Put your hands in (wash them first) and squeeze. Make it cry uncle. Make it say the *Shema*. Liquid is the enemy up to a point. And then it's your friend. Your latke needs a little, but only a little.

› Put the drained ingredients in the mixing bowl. Crack the eggs into the bowl and mix everything together using your wooden spoon.

› Fold in your dry ingredients (spices, salt, etc.). If you were to throw the batter at the wall, it shouldn't drip down, but sort of stick.

› Meanwhile, you've been heating your skillet (iron, remember?). Don't even think about putting in the oil until water droplets dance the kazatsky.

› Pour in one-half cup olive oil. Then pour in the other half.

› Let the oil heat, but don't let it smoke. Smoking's bad for its health.

› Take a deep breath. Do some deep knee bends. Take your spatula off safety.

› Dripping the big metal serving spoon into your batter, drop a big spoonful of batter into the oil. Like you're patting the head of an infant, pat the top of the batter with the spoon so that it spreads out evenly.

› Cook about 4-5 latkes in the skillet at one time. Let them fry. Let them sizzle. Let them bubble.

› Wait two minutes then flip one. You know you want to.

It won't hurt anyone. No one needs to know. Just do it. Is it golden brown? Do you see the face of Moses? Can you sell it on eBay?

› Let it cook on the other side. For every yin there's a yang.

› Pop it on the paper towel you've spread on the baking sheet, which you leave in the oven on warm, then serve with applesauce and sour cream.

Are your guests happy? Are you happy? Is Hanukkah happy?

Yes, it is! Happy Hanukkah!

— *Aaron B. Cohen*

* * *

Can you guess which is the best of all holidays? Hanukkah, of course. Mother is in the kitchen rendering goose fat and frying pancakes. You eat pancakes every day.

— *Shalom Aleichem*

Hanukkah is always a big deal at our house. We like teaching about important holidays (that is, holidays that commemorate historical events) and, of course, holidays that involve light and fire are right up my alley. Growing up, the really special celebrations were at the home of my grandparents, Sam and Ethel Raichlen. We'd light the candles, get gelt, make latkes—the usual but oh, so precious stuff.

On the other side of my family, my Greek Aunt Rosa, would make *zvingos*, a sort of fritter doused with syrup.

More recently, we've had a tradition of going to Sammy's Romanian in New York's Lower East Side for Hanukkah. Our son lives in New York. We all love the free-for-all Bar Mitzvah ambiance of Sammy's and there's nothing like drinking iced vodka to cut the fat in the latkes.

Professionally, as a food writer, I've had an interesting relationship with Hanukkah. In the 1990s, I wrote a series of books about low-fat cooking (to solve a cholesterol problem acquired by reviewing restaurants for *Boston Magazine* in the 1980s). I developed a technique called "bake-frying," in which you'd bake the latkes on a non-stick baking sheet with extra virgin olive oil for flavor. It's profiled in my book, *Healthy Jewish Cooking.* I used Yukon gold potatoes, which have a richer flavor than the usual spuds. These latkes were a big hit with my daughter, Betsy Berthin, who is a dietician, and thus very into low-fat food.

After that, I wrote a book called *Miami Spice,* about Florida's tropical cuisine. That led to latkes made with sweet potato, yam, boniato, and malanga—the latter tropical roots. The applesauce of yore became mango and papaya salsas.

Now we're back to conventional fried latkes, but with locally grown heirloom potatoes, with a few bake-fried for our daughter. We now have grandchildren, so we always make it a point to retell the Hanukkah story, which after all is about redemption, purification, hope, and light in the midst of darkness.

No latkes on the grill for the moment, but our main course is usually smoked brisket. We serve smoked brisket for every holiday.

— *Steven Raichlen*

When I think of latkes, it's the vision of my father standing at the stove that comes to mind. He was robust with an apron stretched over his rotund torso. I can see him slightly flushed as he stood with his spatula before two sizzling, dueling pans and some 20 pounds of potatoes.

After the deed was completed, he would dive right into the massive cleanup. The splattered oil reached every corner of the kitchen.

— *Terri E. Jonisch*

Traditional Latkes
Sheila Weinberg

3 large potatoes (about 1 pound)
½ tsp. salt and ⅛ tsp. pepper
2 eggs
¼ cup finely chopped onion
3 tbsp. flour
1 tbsp. finely chopped parsley
vegetable oil

1. Peel the potatoes and rinse them in cold water. Grate very fine. Place grated potatoes in a colander and run cold water over them. (This will keep potatoes from turning dark.) Using your hands, squeeze out all the water.

2. In a large bowl, beat the eggs. Add the onion, parsley, salt, pepper, and flour. Stir. Add grated potatoes and mix well.

3. Heat a small amount of oil to sizzling in a large frying pan. Drop pancake mixture by the soupspoon full into oil and flatten slightly. Cook until golden brown underneath, turn, and cook on the other side till browned.

4. Eat while still tender but crisp! Latkes are traditionally served with applesauce and/or sour cream.

famous potato pancakes
Bernard Schimmel and Mary Bernstein

¼ cup milk
2 eggs
3 cups diced raw potatoes
1 small onion quartered
3 tbsp. flour
1 tsp. salt
¼ tsp. baking powder

Put all ingredients in blender in order listed and run for about 10 seconds. Do not over blend. Put small amounts onto a hot, greased griddle or fry pan. Fry until brown on both sides.

You can do them ahead and reheat in a hot oven for a few minutes.

zucchini latkes
Sally Marcus

4 cups zucchini, grated
1 cup chopped parsley
1 tsp. lemon pepper
¼ tsp. salt
2 eggs
Oil for frying

In a large bowl mix together all ingredients except oil. Drop by tablespoonful to form 3-inch latkes and fry in hot oil till brown on both sides. Yield approximately 12.

spicy sweet potato latkes
Sophia Ginsberg

3 sweet potatoes, baked, peeled, and mashed
¼ tsp. cumin
½ red onion, diced
¼ tsp. ginger
2 eggs
2 tbsp. cilantro, chopped
Salt to taste
¼ tsp. crushed hot peppers
½ tsp. orange zest
2 tsp. matzah meal

Blend all ingredients together. In large skillet, heat about ½ inch of oil. Drop by tablespoon full. Press batter down with spatula. Fry until brown on one side, then turn and brown other side. Drain on paper towels.

Serve with sour cream.

spinach cheese latkes
Susan Goodman

1 carton frozen spinach
2 cups shredded cheddar cheese
6 eggs
1 cup flour
1 cup milk
Oil as needed

Defrost spinach and squeeze moisture out. Place spinach in blender and add all remaining ingredients except oil. Blend on low until completely combined. Fry latkes in hot oil till brown on both sides.

cottage cheese Latkes
Harriet Weiss

1 cup flour
4 eggs beaten
1 tbsp. sugar
2 cups small curd cottage cheese
1 tsp. baking powder
1 tsp. salt
Oil

Heat oil in pan. Mix dry ingredients, then stir in eggs and cottage cheese. Drop by heaping tablespoon into hot skillet. Turn once, till brown on both sides. Serve with sour cream, applesauce, or fruit jellies.

New Mexico's Finest Hatch Green Chile Latkes with Cilantro Sour Cream

Wendy Katzman

2 lbs. Idaho potatoes
1 large yellow onion
2 eggs
1/3 cup matzah meal
1 tsp. baking powder
1 tsp. salt
Dash of black pepper
½ cup chopped Hatch Green Chilies
Peanut Oil for frying

Cilantro Sour Cream (can be made up to one day ahead)
1 8-oz. carton sour cream (light is fine)
½ cup chopped cilantro
1 large clove of garlic, chopped
Juice of one lime
Salt and pepper to taste

Use a hand grater or food processor to shred potatoes. Place shredded potatoes in a bowl of cold water; shred onion and add to the bowl. Let stand for 30 minutes. You could use the pre-shredded potatoes in the bags. You will need two for this recipe. Chop onion and add to the bowl of potatoes.

Add eggs, matzah meal, baking powder, salt, pepper and chilies. Mix well.

Heat oil in a 10-12 inch frying pan, approximately ½ inch of oil; bring to medium-high heat. Oil is ready when the surface ripples slightly.

Shape latke mixture into 3-inch cakes and place in oil, using a spatula. Fry until the edges are crisp and the inside is golden brown, 3-5 minutes per side. Transfer to paper towels to drain; then put on oven-safe plate and keep warm in the oven on 200° F. while you cook remaining latkes.

Place two to three latkes on a plate with a dollop of cilantro sour cream and if you are feeling indulgent, a pinch of caviar.

asparagus latkes
Kimberly Epstein

1 bunch fresh asparagus, steamed and chopped
1 carrot shredded
1 egg yolk
2 egg whites
¼ each salt, pepper, allspice, marjoram, nutmeg
1 tsp. olive oil
1 tbsp. parsley
1½ tsp. minced garlic
¼ cup minced onion
¼ cup mashed dry curd cottage cheese or ricotta
½ cup matzah meal
1/8 tsp. cream of tartar

Oil for frying

Chop asparagus in food processor. Add carrot. Combine egg yolk with seasonings, oil, and parsley. Stir in garlic, onion, and cheese. Combine asparagus and carrot mixture with batter. Add matzah meal. Beat egg whites separately on high speed. Add cream of tartar and continue beating till stiff. Fold into pancakes.

Fry latkes by tablespoonful in hot oil. Brown on both sides.

carrot-Almond Latkes
Ruth Simon

4 large carrots, grated
½ cup blanched almonds, finely grated
2 eggs
½ cup flour
½ tsp. vanilla
3 tbsp. sugar
Oil for frying
Powdered sugar

In a large bowl, mix all the ingredients. Heat vegetable oil. Scoop out a tablespoon of the mixture and drop into the oil. Flatten the patty in the pan. Cook until golden and flip to the other side. Continue cooking until both sides are brown. Drain on paper towels. Sprinkle with powdered sugar.

moroccan Laatkes
Deborah Safir

4 large boiled potatoes, mashed
2 large eggs
¼ lb. grated parmesan cheese
1-2 tbsp. flour
2 tbsp. fresh minced parsley
Salt and pepper to taste
Breadcrumbs or flour for frying

Combine all ingredients. Mix slightly till mixture sticks together.

Use one tablespoon of mixture at a time and pat into round flat shapes. Dip in breadcrumbs or flour mixture and fry till golden.

Makes 2 dozen latkes.

Low-fat Latkes
Carolyn Kaplan

3 large potatoes, peeled and grated
¼ cup grated onion
¼ cup egg substitute (or egg whites only)
½ tsp. salt
¼ tsp. baking powder
3 tbsp. matzah meal

Place grated potatoes in ice water for an hour. Drain well and press out excess moisture. Place in mixing bowl and add onion and egg substitute and mix well. In a small bowl, combine salt, baking powder and matzah meal. Slowly add to potato mixture, mixing very well. Drop by tablespoonful onto hot, lightly oiled or sprayed skillet. Cook on one side until well-browned, turn over and brown other side.

Apple Rum Latkes
Stephanie Albert

2 cups all-purpose flour   3 tsp. baking powder
1 tbsp. sugar   1 tsp. salt
½ tsp. cinnamon   ¼ cup golden raisins
½ cup cider or apple juice   1/3 cup milk
¼ cup rum   2 eggs
2 tbsp. vegetable shortening   Cinnamon sugar to sprinkle
1 red apple, unpeeled, cored, sliced in wafer-thin wedges
Oil for frying

In a bowl, combine flour, baking powder, salt, vegetable shortening, sugar, cinnamon and raisins. Make a well in the center and add cider or apple juice, milk, brandy and eggs. Stir to mix.

Heat oil in a large skillet over medium heat until a drop of mixture sizzles. Drop 2 tablespoonful of mixture for each latke into hot oil. Place 2 to 3 apple wedges on top. Flatten slightly with the back of a wooden spoon. Fry over medium heat for 2 to 3 minutes longer until the second side is nicely browned. Serve hot, sprinkled with cinnamon sugar.

chocolate chip latkes
Melissa Levin

3 ½ cups semi-sweet chocolate chips, slightly melted
4 egg whites
3 cups shredded coconut
6 tbsp. sugar
2 tsp. vanilla
Touch of salt

Preheat oven to 350° F, line cookie sheets with parchment paper.

Combine all ingredients in stainless steel mixing bowl.

Put bowl in large pan of slowly simmering water and stir, scraping, until sticky and hot.

Put by rounded tablespoonful about 2 inches apart on cookie sheets. Flatten each cookie with fingers so they're the size of small latkes.

Bake 13-15 minutes, till golden brown. Cool completely before removing from parchment.

Latkes are a favorite hanukkah food, linked to hanukkah because of the oil. our family, however, has a special reason. my father was ready to propose to my mother on their third date. he was quite certain he wanted to marry this wonderful woman, but he had to be absolutely sure, so he asked the key question as they rowed around the central park lake: "can you make latkes?" "sure," said my mother-to-be. "perfect," thought my father to himself: "well, then will you marry me?" and they lived happily ever after.

— *Blu Greenberg*

Latkes, Jewish Weapons of Mass Destruction, are pancake-like structures not to be confused with anything a first-class health restaurant would serve. In a latke, the oil remains inside the pancake. It could be used to shine your shoes or lubricate your automobile. There is a rumor that in the time of the Maccabees, they lit a latke by mistake, and it burned for eight months. What is certain is that you will have heartburn for at least the same amount of time.

— *Synagogue Bulletin*

8

Let my people enjoy

According to tradition, Hanukkah is a holiday of joy, laughter, and celebration

Do not fast during Hanukkah,
not on the day preceding
nor yet on the day following.
Eat and be merry.
Linger over your viands,
punctuate your meals with jest and song,
Relate miracles.

— *Code of Rabbinical Judaism*

LET MY PEOPLE ENJOY

Shirley was giving directions to her grandson who was coming to her new apartment for dinner on the first night of Hanukkah. She said, "Come to the front door of the apartment building. I'm in 19D. There's a big panel at the door. Push button 19D with your elbow. Then I'll buzz you in.

Come inside. The elevator is on the right. Get in, and with your elbow hit 19.

When you get out, I'm on the right. Then with your elbow, hit my doorbell."

"Okay, Grandma, I'll do it, but why am I hitting all those buttons with my elbow?"

"You're coming empty-handed?"

— *Synagogue Bulletin*

Let me tell you the one thing
i have against moses. he took
us 40 years into the desert
in order to bring us
to the one place in the
middle east that has no oil.

— *Golda Meir*

Ben dies and goes to heaven. The first person he sees is his beloved old teacher, Rabbi Morris. But he was stunned to see the rabbi, sitting in a leopard brocaded chair, with a former lady of the evening in his lap.

"Rabbi, how could you?" asked Ben. "You were always the most righteous man. You conducted Shabbat services, led the Hanukkah blessings. What happened? Is she your reward for living such an honorable life?"

"No, Ben, she is not my reward," explained the rabbi. "I'm her punishment."

— *Edward Bernstein*

The maccabees won, and they went to the temple. Then the animals went to the bathroom. After that the maccabees cleaned up, and then they found the oil and lit the menorah. That's the story of the maccabees.

— *Nina Pickus, age 4.*

Five-year-old zachary was confused. His mother told him they didn't believe in christmas, and they didn't believe in santa claus.

Thinking this over, he asked, "Do we believe in winter?"

— *Phyllis Hirsch*

top five reasons to like hanukkah

Never a silent night when you're with your family

No roof damage from reindeer

fun waxy build up on the menorah

If someone forgets a gift, there are 7 days to correct it

No awkward explanation of the virgin birth

Hanukkah represents freedom for all Jews. The festival of Lights is a miracle because we thought we only had enough oil for one night. somehow it lasted eight nights. Luckily, the Arabs weren't in charge of the oil at the time. — *Jackie Mason*

what Bloomberg wants for the eight Days of Hanukkah

1. A third term
2. For people to forget how he was able to run for a third term
3. For Christine Quinn to stop dropping by the house at all hours "just to talk" and check what's in the fridge
4. A Lexington Avenue subway spur leading straight to his Upper East Side townhouse
5. A musical about his mayoralty, like LaGuardia and Koch got
6. An invitation to stay in the Lincoln Bedroom
7. To become a Democrat again, now that the Republican and Independent things aren't working for him
8. "What do you mean there are only eight days to Hanukkah? Can't City Council do something about that?"

— *Synagogue Bulletin*

I sometimes think that god, in creating man, somewhat overestimated His ability.

— *Oscar Wilde*

you might be a jewish redneck if...

1. Your belt buckle is bigger than your yarmulke
2. You light your Hanukkah candles with your cigarette
3. Instead of a noisemaker, you've fired a shotgun at the sound of Haman's name
4. You have a gun rack in your Sukkah
5. You think "KKK" is a symbol for really kosher
6. You think marrying your first cousin is required according to Jewish law
7. You are saving a bottle of Mogen David wine for a special occasion
8. And when someone shouts L'chaim, you respond L'howdy

— *Synagogue Bulletin*

The greatest Jewish tradition is to laugh. The cornerstone of Jewish survival has always been to find humor in life and in ourselves.

— *Jerry Seinfeld*

Six-year-old Olivia was having dinner at her grandma's house the first night of Hanukkah. When everyone sat down, and the food was served, she began eating.

Her mom said, "Sweetheart, we have to wait till we say the prayer."

"I don't have to," Olivia piped up.

"Dear, don't we always say a prayer before we eat at our house?"

"Yes," Olivia answered, "but this is Grandma's house. She knows how to cook."

— *Patty Leventhall*

Whoever is happy will make others happy, too. He who has courage and faith will never perish in misery.

— *Anne Frank*

Judaism teaches that you will be held accountable for every delight you see that you did not participate in. god made a world of good things. part of appreciating god is appreciating god's world.

— *Rabbi David Wolpe*

glossary

Bubbe	Grandmother
Cantor	Synagogue's music leader
Challah	Special bread for Shabbat and festivals
Cholent	Traditional stew cooked slowly overnight
Daven	To pray
D'var Torah	A word of Torah, relating to portion of the week
Dreidel	Spinning top of 4 sides
Erev	Night before a holiday
Gelt	Hanukkah money, often chocolate coins
Haftorah	The book of the prophets
Hallel	Seasonal blessing
Hanukkah	Eight Day Feast of Dedication
Havura	A group that prays and studies together

Hazzan	Hebrew word for Cantor
Kiddush	Blessing over wine
Latkes	A traditional Hanukkah potato pancake
Maoz Tzur	Hanukkah song "Rock of Ages"
Matzah balls	Balls cooked with matzah meal and eggs and served in soup
Menorah	Candelabrum of nine branches used for Hanukkah
Mohel	Jewish person trained to perform circumcisions
Oy Vey	Exclamation of dismay
Rosh Hashanah	Jewish New Year
Shabbat	Sabbath, day of rest
Shalom	Hello or peace or good-bye
Shamash	The service candle that lights the other candles on the menorah

Shaharit	Morning prayer service
Shema	Prayer affirming the belief in one God
Shiva	Mourning period of seven days
Shochet	A person trained to slaughter animals and birds in a Kosher way
Sukkot	One of three pilgrimage festivals
Sufganiyot	Jelly donuts eaten during Hanukkah
Talmud	Torah commentaries
Tchotchkes	Inexpensive trinkets
Torah	First five books of the Hebrew Bible
Tzedakah	Righteousness, commonly referred to as charity
Yom Kippur	Day of Attonement
Zayde	Grandfather
Zmirot	Jewish hymms

acknowledgements

My sincere thanks and appreciation go to the one and only Ozzie Nogg, a mentor, a colleague, an editor extraordinaire, but most importantly, a friend.

This book would not have been possible without the wonderful contributions of Dominique Tomasov Binder, www.urbancultours.com; Aaron B. Cohen, Executive Editor, JUF News, the amazing Joanie Jacobson, my smart, talented niece Abigail Pickus, Steven Raichlen, www.barbequebible.com; Mordechai M. Schmutter, author of *Don't Yell "Challah" in a Crowded Matzah Bakery*; Scott D. Strawn of the *Island Packet*, and the U.S. Holocaust Memorial Museum.

I am always thankful to have the two finest daughters I could wish for: Wendy Katzman and Amy Levine.

A portion of the profits
from this book are being donated to
The Kripke Federation Jewish Library
in Omaha, Nebraska.

A portion of the profits
from this book are being donated to
The Kripke Federation Jewish Library
in Omaha, Nebraska.